[Ø]THE OWNED

PROGRAMMED TO
FAIL

How to Break Through Your
Mental Blocks and **Achieve Greatness**

BRANDON EPSTEIN

I'D LIKE TO DEDICATE THIS BOOK FIRST AND FOREMOST TO SENSEI CLAY.

My brother and mentor who started me down the path of personal awakening and has shared with me many of the tools and frameworks that you will find within this book. I also would like to dedicate this book to my family and friends who make Heaven on Earth possible for me through their love and support. Mainly my wife Sara and my parents Benj and Joann who have given me the unconditional love and permission to be the fullest expression of myself. Finally to my daughters Mar and Luna, who I hope will one day be able to embody the wisdom in this book in a way that allows them to live a life full of joy and purpose.

CONTENTS

INTRODUCTION
TRUTH SEEKERS START HERE

EFORE I START BERATING YOU WITH WHAT'S BROKEN, let me first congratulate you on what's working. The only reason you picked up this book is because you're a genuine seeker of truth. Undoubtedly you have already unlocked a tremendous amount of your potential. This book is a guide to capitalizing on all the hard work you have already put in. Trust that all you need to achieve your version of greatness is already within you right now. No matter your goal or your circumstances, together we will make the necessary upgrades to your underlying mental programming to unleash your full potential. Here are just a few examples from my personal clients who went through the same process you are about to embark on.

An NFL player, fresh off a 30-million-dollar contract, was ready to call it quits because he was so afraid of the judgment he would receive from coaches, management, the fan base, and media if he didn't live up to the hype of his contract. By rewiring his subconscious, using the techniques you're about to learn, he went from dreading his career to loving his career, becoming one of the best players on his team, and being motivated to play for another ten-plus years.

A CEO of a major sports agency was unable to let go of the operations of his company, and it was costing him his health, mental peace, and money. By rewiring his subconscious, we were able to release him from working out of obligation so that he could tap fully into his unique talents. By doing so, his work became more fun than ever, and he launched a passion project that generated an extra $8 million in unexpected revenue that year for his business.

A shy young man with a safe job had always dreamed about being a keynote speaker but was deathly afraid of talking in public around anyone besides his close friends. I helped him rewire his subconscious in a way that empowered him to find his voice and start speaking his truth. He was able to embrace the vulnerabilities that used to make him feel ashamed, and this led to him booking his first TEDx keynote.

A lawyer-client of mine was unable to deal with the stress of a toxic work environment and was constantly being torn down by an overly judgmental and fearful family. Through rewiring his subconscious, we were able to free him from the self-sabotaging programming that gave those people power over his emotions. He can now stand in the eye of the storm, unflinching and peaceful, regardless of any circumstance.

A college basketball player was overwhelmed by the pressure she felt from an overbearing coach who was sabotaging her ability to be herself and play her best. Through rewiring her subconscious to create an inner world of peace and resilience, she was able to transcend the obstacles on her team to unlock her best performances and a career in professional basketball.

A professional boxer who would dominate anyone he faced in sparring would show up as a shell of himself and lose the major fights that would land him a world title shot. By rewiring his subconscious to make him believe he was worthy of the success he desired, we unlocked the killer instinct that lay dormant inside of him. By doing so, he was able to win the biggest fight of his career, securing a secondary world title belt.

The commonality between all these client success stories is that they had already achieved a measure of success before they worked with me. They had the potential to be world-class, but there were deficiencies in their subconscious programming that were causing them to suppress their full capacity for greatness. Immediately upon rewiring their subconscious minds, the life created by the mental roadblocks that used to hold them back instantly vanished. They were able to embrace who they had always been beneath their hidden self-limiting programming. The beautiful part of all their journeys is that they didn't have to become anything that they were not. Instead, they just had to reclaim the energy that was holding them back so they could fully step into their power and into a life in flow.

Throughout this journey together, I am going to hold you to the same high standard that I hold my personal clients to. In doing so, you will be inspired to expand your perception of reality and what you believe is possible. I know you can do this because you've done it before. That's how you got here. You have been relentlessly seeking new ways to expand your abilities and potential. The process is always the same. You find out what's holding you back, you acknowledge that there is room to grow, and then you learn the skills and put in the repetitions to get where you want to go. Okay, enough of the pep talk. Let's talk business.

You have been programmed to fail.

Not just you, but everyone. On average, 80 percent of people's thoughts are negative. Ninety-five percent of those thoughts are recurring daily. We get stuck with the same negative thinking and the corresponding bad habits playing on a loop because we are unconscious of how we were programmed in the first place.

If you're like 99.99 percent of people out there, you have been trying to fix your problems with your conscious rational mind. Pure force and will. This will work up to a point, but if we want to push you to the next level, we are going to need to upgrade your mental strategy to get results. You see, your conscious mind maxes out at a processing power of around 40 bits of information per second. Whereas your subconscious mind can process over 40 million bits of information per second.[1]

---

1   To put this into context, think about your conscious mind as the awareness of thoughts and feelings in the present moment. Your subconscious mind is storing all the information that produces those feelings and thoughts. For example, you may have a special memory of dancing to a specific song with someone you love. When that song plays on the radio while you're driving, your conscious mind hears and recognizes it, and then your subconscious brings awareness to the thoughts and feelings associated with that song.

You may be thinking to yourself, *Well, I've done pretty damn well using my conscious mind,* and to that, I say, "Imagine what would be possible if you fully tapped into the subconscious supercomputer that drives all your thoughts, feelings, and behavior from beneath the conscious surface."

The answer is exponential results in all aspects of your life.

UNLOCKING YOUR SUBCONSCIOUS MIND

What I've found with the professional athletes, business executives, creative artists, and other high achievers I've worked with is that most of us are programmed to succeed in one or a few areas of life. Maybe on paper, you have a successful career, maybe you have a surplus of cash in the bank, maybe you're ripped with six-pack abs, maybe you have an amazing circle of loving relationships in your life, and maybe you live in a state of perpetual inner peace.

Despite crushing it in one or more areas in your life, I imagine that there is at least one area where you are sucking at or at least underperforming in. Well, even if that area you suck in doesn't seem like a top priority, it sabotages your ability to reach your full potential and, most importantly, feel your best.

For example, I find that when a pro athlete or successful CEO comes to me to work on improving performance in their career, we end up tackling the areas they are weak in, because it becomes blatantly apparent how their hidden weaknesses end up draining their biological battery and leaving them with less capacity to tackle their career.

The core of the work we will be doing together is centered around the hidden subconscious programming within your mind. Every repeating negative thought or habit stems from a piece of subconscious programming that is in your mind and needs to be pulled out to create space for something new to emerge. The truth is you don't have to become anything you're not. At your core, you are the person you need to be already. I'm just going to help you get rid of your extra baggage so you can run farther, faster, and with more joy. We all suck at something, and if you are willing to humble yourself, you can find out how you were programmed to fail in those areas that you're stuck in so you can reclaim that energy and turn it into personal power and success in every aspect of your life.

OWNING YOUR FOCUS AND CHOICES

This book is not for everyone. Most people have no interest in going through the grueling process explained here. This book has been written for the exceptional people out there who are sick of quick fixes and magic-pill promises and want an actual framework for mastering their inner and outer world for the rest of their lives. It's not easy—trust me, I've been through it. But what'd you expect? You don't build a body capable of performing at an elite level without doing the hard work. You don't build a multi-million-dollar business without doing the hard work. You don't build deep, meaningful, lasting relationships without investing heavily in them.

Taking back the power of your inner world is the same. You need to build your inner world so it becomes your inner paradise. Only there will you experience true freedom. To do so, you will need to take ownership of only two things: your focus and your choices.

Imagine this. You are a human vessel receiving and being powered by the energy of the universe. That energy is flowing through you in every moment and is being directed based on where you choose to focus and what you choose to do. Believe it or not, your choices are actually just a byproduct of your focus because wherever you are focused (consciously or unconsciously) will determine where you feel intrinsic motivation to take action.

The road map I'll be sharing on our journey together has been designed to systematically audit the way you focus (consciously and unconsciously) so you can transmute what's been holding you back into what will inevitably push you forward. And just as you must own your focus, you will need to own your choices in a way that has you step into your power instead of playing the victim. Being a victim will give you short-term emotional relief but will ultimately stunt your growth and limit your potential. Conversely, being the victor means you own every aspect of your life and are willing to alchemize your pain into your power.

Owning your focus and choices is a lifestyle. It's a way of being where you can easily set GPS coordinates for yourself in life—like career goals, income goals, physical health goals, or relationships goals—and achieve them without any inner resistance working against you. Does that mean you won't have to work hard? Fuck no! What it means is that you won't be slowed down or held back by worrying about other people's opinions, self-doubt, regret, anxiety, overwhelming stress, and all the other nonsense that previously clouded your mind and made it hard to get clarity on the correct course of action. You also won't be dealing with the negative feelings that lead to self-sabotaging thoughts and inconsistent actions. Instead, you will be able to stay consistent all the way through the finish line, because you have been hard-wired for success. Being consistent becomes the only viable path forward.

If you can own your focus and choices, you're going to learn a hell of a lot from my story (Part 1) and will be empowered to utilize the tools I present to you in my personal playbook for peak performance and peak human experience (Part 2).

MEET YOUR GUIDE

So why trust me as your guide?

Well, I've been in the shit pit. As you'll learn in my story, I was programmed to believe I was a worthless piece of shit, which meant that I didn't believe I was worthy of any of the goals I set for myself. From my physical health—to my peace of mind—to financial abundance—to a rewarding career—to amazing relationships—you name it, and I was programmed to fail at it. By the age of seven, I had been through sexual trauma and was full of anger and insecurity. By twenty, I was hypertensive and fifty pounds overweight. By twenty-four, I was $80,000 in credit card debt, unemployed, and forced to sublet my apartment and move down to South America.

I had to go on the inner journey to reprogram myself to succeed, and as I've done so, I've achieved many of my wildest dreams: from becoming a mental performance coach to the world's best pro athletes—to growing a wellness community with over a million members—to building a seven-figure business—to living in a physically powerful body—to creating heaven on earth through my own family—to surrounding myself with an amazing group of friends—to most importantly *becoming meditation*. When you become meditation, it means you have the heightened state of awareness and skills to shift your emotional state of being in any given moment so you can transmute your inner resistance into inner motivation and momentum—so you can feel and perform your best in any situation.

It's taken me fifteen years of working on myself and in the field of mental performance to gain the wisdom I'll be sharing through my story and frameworks, so let's just say I've already done most of the heavy lifting and suffering to figure this stuff out. Now, you can learn from my mistakes and take the clear-cut path to success that I am laying out for you.

YOUR ROAD MAP

There are two parts to this book. Part one is where I share stories from my personal life with you, so you can see the journey I went on to gain these skills and how they have created real-world results in my life. I will also be sharing stories of my clients, that range from college students to pro athletes to entry-level employees to eight-figure CEOs, so you can learn how these skills work for anyone, no matter their circumstance. You'll notice a fair number of stories that relate to success in sports. I have included those because sports are a perfect metaphor for life. Each of us is embarking on our own personal mission, and sports make that mission black and white. Whether you want success in business, sports, art, or anything else, you will have to face your inner resistance along the way.

In Part 2, I will lay out my entire playbook for you, so you can own these skills yourself and reprogram yourself to step into your highest potential. If you learn best by watching videos, I've also provided my online owned training course that includes full-length videos to guide you through everything you will read about in the playbook. This is available on my website *www.theowned.industries/training*.

Before we begin this journey, I cannot overstate enough how powerful an undertaking this process is. Most people don't make it through this process because it requires tremendous discipline and courage—again, as does achieving anything in the top 1 percent of any field. Hall of Fame athletes are not normal people. Having a net worth over seven figures is not normal. Living in a state of consistent peace is not normal. Being physically elite is not normal. Having incredible relationships that empower you to be your best is not normal. Now one or more of these things might be normal for you, but I'm sure the path you took to make it your normal *was not normal!*

You took abnormal levels of action and held yourself to abnormal standards to get to where you are today. This is a book for those seekers of truth out there who don't give a fuck about the status quo and are constantly looking for ways to live their most extraordinary life while sharing their unique talents, regardless of what other people are saying or doing.

If you are willing to move through the discomfort to awaken to your full potential, then this book is for you, and I couldn't be more excited to start this journey with you.

Warning, I am not a normal dude, so the depth of vulnerability that I will share through my stories will not be normal. I'm going to share exactly how I went from the darkest of the dark to the lightest of the light without any censoring of the truth.

Let's begin.

PART 1

THE STORY

Part 1 of this book is designed to build trust between the two of us. I don't know about you, but I would never take advice from someone who I don't respect and believe in. By sharing my stories of personal struggle and triumph, I hope to earn your respect and enough belief in my process for rewiring your subconscious mind to have you execute the road map I lay out for you in Part 2 of this book. The first step is believing it's possible, and that belief will be ingrained in you through the stories I'll share from my personal life in Part 1. Furthermore, it's hard for the rational mind to understand how the subconscious works because most of the time it's completely hidden from our awareness. In each of my stories, I'll be connecting the lessons learned to the underlying subconscious programming that eventually led to my success and the success of my clients. So, in summary, the journey you are about to go on looks like this. Part 1 will ingrain within you the WHY you should do this, which will fuel you with the motivation and inspiration to execute the HOW in Part 2.

CHAPTER 1
THIS IS HOW YOU WERE PROGRAMMED

B Y THE TIME WE ARE ADULTS, we have already received the majority of the subconscious programming that shapes our identities. Our identity cradles the person we are and how we show up in the world. None of us consciously choose our identity because we don't choose our programming. The majority of our programming is a direct reflection of the community we grow up around, the experiences we have had, and the unconscious generational beliefs that our parents have un-knowingly passed along to us. Some programming works for us, some work against us, and some is generally benign. The programming that works against us can be very sneaky because oftentimes it can make us feel bad for no rational reason and can lead to poor decision-making that holds us back from achieving our goals.

Can you remember a time in your life when you said or did some-thing irrational that sabotaged a relationship or a goal that you had? The rational part of you would have never done that, but the unseen programming beneath the surface created an emotional experience that blinded you from seeing the bigger picture.

What's important to remember about our programming is that it is contextual to our own lived experience. The worst thing to ever happen to you is the worst thing to ever happen to you. The resulting subcon-scious self-limiting programming can have a tremendous effect on you even if you rationally perceive your trauma to be less than someone else's. You can't compare your experience to anyone else's, because the way you perceive the world is fundamentally different.

You have countless subconscious programs all running at the same time, and the truth is that none of the programming is designed to make you fail. It's actually designed to help you survive. Unfortunately, when you are striving toward elite levels of performance, you need to go beyond survival. Your goal is to thrive. That is why you must release yourself from old programming that no longer serves you, so you can replace it with new programming that will align with your new personal goals. Think about it like outgrowing clothes from childhood. The clothes may have fit you as a child, but they are not going to fit you as you continue to grow.

SELF-LIMITING SUBCONSCIOUS PROGRAMMING

I'm sitting in tenth grade European History class, and Mr. Stewart calls on me for my opinion on *The Iliad* by Homer. Instantly my face turns beet red, my heart starts beating out of my chest, and I freeze like a deer in headlights.

"Uh. Uh." *Say something. ANYTHING!* I think to myself. I start sweating and thinking about how every kid in the class is probably wondering why this kid's face is so red. I freeze up and draw a complete blank on what *The Iliad* is even about. I mumble something in response to his question, and he kindly moves on (seeing that I am obviously suffering and in no way capable of having a coherent conversation).

The discussion moves on beyond me, my heart starts to beat slower, and slowly my face goes from red to pink and then back to pale again. Immediately, my mind starts racing about how everyone in the class (mainly the cute girls) probably think I'm a complete weirdo for getting so embarrassed over a simple question.

That example is a symptom of poor subconscious programming. A little bit of pressure was applied, and my ability to perform went out the window. It had nothing to do with what I knew or didn't know. It had everything to do with my lack of self-worth, stemming from underlying programming that made me think that I wasn't worth shit.

To be honest, no one was using the word anxiety at that time, so I didn't even know what the overwhelming feeling was. All I knew was that when pressure crept in, the version of me that performed well in any aspect of life disappeared and was replaced by an overly anxious version of me that was frozen in fear. In hindsight, I can see that there were two versions of me. The real deep down version of me that was cool and confident when I wasn't under pressure and a version of me that would make me freeze up and underperform whenever the pressure was on.

What I now know is that I was living with an identity that was not in alignment with who I wanted to be. Our identity is stored beneath the conscious surface in the form of our subconscious programming. That programming is a byproduct of genetic and lived experiences that create this experience of "me." For better or worse, we will always do things in alignment with who we believe we are. The identity I had at the beginning of my journey did not allow me to perform under pressure because my subconscious programming was in conflict with my conscious desires. That identity and the corresponding programming stemmed from life experiences that I had up until that point and core conditioning I had received from my family, friends, and overall cultural upbringing (more on that later). Poor programming presents itself most when we are under pressure and leads to us running into invisible walls that hold us back from being who we truly are.

Extrapolating this out, we see this in high achievers all the time. It's the reason a wide receiver drops a potentially game-winning catch that they would normally make 99/100 in practice. It's the reason why a basketball player gets into a slump at the free throw line in games despite their ability to sink 90 percent of their free throws in practice. It's the reason why a business owner makes an impulsive decision that sabotages a business relationship. It's the reason a musician takes five years to put out their sophomore album after their debut album is a massive success. It's almost never a talent issue. It's about our ability to execute when we encounter our own inner resistance—resistance being another code word for self-limiting subconscious programming.

Self-limiting programming can surface in all sorts of unusual ways, and many of us experience the full gambit of them during our teenage and young adult years when our bodies and minds are going through the most growth and development. Speaking from experience, I had all kinds of weird physical things that would pop up for me ranging from random warts I would get on my hands—to chronic dandruff—to acne—to oily and peeling skin—to having trouble getting my dick hard or orgasming with a woman—to freezing up with a red face and paralyzed mind when experiencing any substantial pressure. These physical issues were caused by intense stress and anxiety, which have all been linked to the issues listed above. When we are able to better program ourselves, the stress and anxiety disappear and lead to fewer physical symptoms. Sure, many of these symptoms are common among teenagers, but I would argue that most teenagers are dealing with unresolved traumas and many of these ailments could be avoided if the underlying self-defeating programming is transmuted to work for them instead of against them.

CORE WOUNDS

When we are unconscious of our suppressed underlying programming that stems from a traumatic event, something called a "core wound" can emerge. This core wound creates self-sabotaging programming that often leads to us acting out in the world in a way that is not in alignment with the person we want to be.

After working with hundreds of one-on-one clients, it is apparent to me that everyone has some sort of core wound.

Even you. Even if you can't name it right now.

Some core wounds come from sexual abuse.

Some core wounds come from physical abuse.

Some core wounds come from verbal abuse.

Some core wounds just come from witnessing something traumatizing.

Core wounds come in many different forms, but the resulting trauma has the same effect on all of us. They imprint a self-limiting program deep into our subconscious that prevents us from being, feeling, and performing our best. They leave us with this underlying feeling of **who I am is not enough**.

Whether you have uncovered your core wound or not doesn't matter. You don't actually need to know what your core wound is to resolve it. You just need to recognize that the negative patterns of thinking and behavior stem from the imprinting you received at a young age and you have the power to change it. If you have the courage to go into the darkness and uncover the self-limiting programming that stems from that core wound, you can transmute that programming so it moves you toward the life you want instead of holding you back from it.

As we will get into later in this book, not all self-limiting programming stems from your core wound, but it can definitely be a catalyst for poor programming to manifest later in life. The reason core wounds are so impactful is that they happen during our primary programming years (between birth and seven) when we are learning how to survive in our tribe.

Throughout high school, I did have a couple of events happen that gave me a glimpse at an underlying unconscious core wound that I had yet to deal with. One night I had a couple of my guy friends and a couple of my girlfriends over to my house to hang out. This was a big deal. Girls in my room. Major score! I was flying high and feeling myself until my twenty-year-old brother burst into the room and exclaimed, "Hey! You know my brother and I had sex with each other!"

"WTF?!" I yelled at him. This triggered the reddest face of all my red faces, and I stumbled over my words to say, "What are you talking about?!" and slammed the door in his face.

You may be wondering what twenty-year-old-man would say such a thing. Well—a very low-functioning twenty-year-old with Down syndrome would. Most people don't know how to deal with people with Down syndrome, so I was able to play it off like, "Yeah, that's just my brother, and he has Down syndrome, sorry about that." The discussion moved on, and no one really thought much of it, but I was devastated internally. When my friends finally left, I had to sit with what my brother had just said, and memories started to flood in from early childhood. The memory that surfaced was from when I was seven years old and my brother was twelve years old and just starting to go through puberty.

Little did I know, but the summer before, my brother had been sexually abused at a sleepaway camp and was trying to cope with that experience. He did so by acting out sexually toward me. His seven-year-old little brother. When my parents were gone for any length of time, he would get naked, rub himself on me and try to do sexual acts that, at the time, I didn't fully understand. I had a feeling that there was something wrong with this but was also curious about the stimulation I would feel when he would do this to me.

He began to consistently act out sexually toward me whenever we were on family trips together and were forced to share a bed. We would get naked and rub our naked bodies against one another for stimulation. This continued on a few occasions until at some point I felt there was something deeply wrong with this and made him stop. By then, it was too late. My core wound had been formed, and I was never the same again.

A child psychologist might have told me this was normal behavior for young kids my age, but I didn't tell anyone about it, and I slowly began to hate myself for what had happened between my brother and me. Yes, I was just seven years old, but at the time, I already believed I was mentally the older brother and set expectations for myself to be the standard for good behavior. I had known from the age of four that I needed to act like the bigger brother, even if my brother was older than me. This recognition led to me believing that I needed to take ownership of everything that happened between us regardless of whose fault it actually was.

After those sexual traumas took place at the age of seven, I pushed them down deep inside of me. I stuffed down the shame and guilt of doing this with my brother, believing it was my fault and that I was to blame for what had happened. I believed I was a bad person. I believed I was wrong. I believed there was something wrong with me, and I believed that I had done something irreversibly wrong that I could never come back from. In hindsight, I can now see that the sexual trauma with my brother was internalized as **my core wound** and would plague me for decades to come.

We live in a society where **most** people are either physically or mentally ill because we suppress our trauma and then act out from a place of fear and insecurity. We don't learn how to resolve trauma so we can live happy and healthy free-flowing lives. Instead, we stuff it down deeper and deeper until that unexpressed energy manifests into poor choices that can ruin our lives before they even get started.

The more I suppressed my trauma and kept it inside, the more anger I felt and acted out. What was buried in my subconscious bubbled up into a need to constantly prove my worth to myself and my peers. This led to me constantly getting into fights with kids in my neighborhood when I was younger. I remember one time (around eleven years old) it got so bad that I literally tackled a kid who was teasing me in the middle of class and started beating on him in a fit of tears before standing on my desk and telling the substitute teacher at the time to go fuck herself. Poor teacher, she had no idea what she got herself into taking on that teaching gig for the day.

This feeling of shame and guilt from the experience with my brother continued to bubble beneath the surface until one day, around the age of eleven, I couldn't take it anymore. I sat my mom down and confessed. I told her about what happened, hoping to clear my conscience. I don't remember the exact conversation, but I do know that it was quick and didn't help me at all. I just kind of remember her silence and acknowledgment. She didn't want to make her mentally disabled son wrong for what happened to me and also didn't know how to put me at ease, so my confession ended up reinforcing my belief that it was, in fact, my fault, and I was a worthless piece of shit for what had happened. It was no fault of my mom's for how I felt. She didn't know how to release me from this suffering, and so we just continued on with family life, business as usual.

The need to prove my worth continued to surface. By the time I was in high school, I began to take lots of drugs and get completely wasted to numb the pain of being me.

One night in particular, when I was sixteen years old, I almost ended my journey before it even got started. My friends and I were partying at a buddy's house, and we ran out of alcohol. I was already completely wasted but volunteered to drive us to the local 7-Eleven to try and find someone to buy us beer. We packed into my mom's Subaru Forester, with five people filling all the open seats and two additional people lying down in the open trunk space.

Two minutes into the drive, we were heading down some back roads where there was a steep incline followed by a mound of concrete. This is the kind of road that you need to go fifteen miles per hour down to make sure your car doesn't go airborne. Instead of slowing down, I thought it would be a good idea to rev the gas and try to launch my car into the air like I was playing a video game. With Gnarls Barkley's "Crazy" blaring in the background, I heard my buddy in the front seat shout, "Hey dude, I think we should slow down!" I yelled back at him, "I do this all the time, relax!" Those were some famous last words. The car lifted into the air, and as we came back down, I lost complete control of the car and tried to hit the brakes to gain back control. It was too late.

Before I knew it, the car spun out 180 degrees, hit a curb, and flipped over onto its side. In slow motion, I remember us all slowly crawling out of the car, and miraculously no one was injured. After what felt like a matter of seconds after the crash, I heard sirens heading our way, and I immediately told my friends to run away—that I would handle the police. When the police arrived, I told them I was going for a joy ride by myself. They found a bong, a random girl's flip-flop, and a bunch of Olde 40s in the backseat.

It was obvious I wasn't by myself, but for whatever reason, I only got a slap on the wrist. The only charge I received was drinking and driving. I was put in a rehabilitation program for the next four months, and after six months, I would have my license reinstated. I wish I could tell you that rehab was an enlightening experience for me, but it wasn't. I didn't receive any tools to do the deeper healing necessary to change my behavior, and by the time I got out, I was the same person I was when I had gone in.

Later on this journey, I will share with you just how simple it can be to do the healing work necessary to avoid making poor choices like this, but unfortunately, these life skills are not taught in most schools or rehabilitation programs. No one forced me into a state of awareness where I could uncover why I was actually doing what I was doing. The answer in this scenario was that I wanted to prove to myself and others that I wasn't weak—that I could be a badass. I couldn't have been more wrong, but it would be years before I would develop the awareness to see the situation clearly.

HOW SUBCONSCIOUS PROGRAMMING WORKS

We've all heard stories of childhood trauma manifesting in dramatic ways later on in life—but why is that? The answer is simple. Survival. We make it through trauma by building subconscious defense and coping mechanisms. These mechanisms, which I will refer to as subconscious self-limiting programming, are good for getting you through the trauma but terrible for empowering you to live a healthy and happy life long-term. Let's talk about the stages of programming that we go through. Every human on earth receives their primary programming for life between the ages of birth to seven. Before seven, your brainwaves are slowed down to a level where you can easily assimilate to your tribe so you can survive and hopefully even thrive. Those brainwave states allow direct access to your subconscious mind and allow for a fluidity in your identity as your lived experience shapes your belief system. During this time, you are literally going through hypnosis. The reason I say hypnosis is because this is the only period of your life where you are in a wildly suggestible state of being. As an adult, you are mostly operating in a beta brainwave state, which makes you think more rationally about things and doesn't allow much access to your subconscious mind, aka the supercomputer that runs your life. Your subconscious holds on to your identity as a whole, which is being shaped by your belief system. By the time you are an adult, most of your beliefs are already formulated and more or less set in stone.

The only way you have access to those hypnotic brainwave states as an adult is when you are sleeping, in deep meditation, or under hypnosis. You will be learning the techniques in Part 2 (Training 13) of this book to get into the necessary meditative states to access your subconscious reliably. Most people never learn how to do this, which is why their programming stays inaccessible throughout the rest of their lives. The truth is through proper meditation techniques, you can incept new beliefs, and through repetition you can ingrain those new beliefs to be a part of your core underlying programming.

That being said, biologically it makes complete sense that we have been wired the way we have. By the time you are an adult, you are supposed to have all the necessary programming needed for survival. That is why when you're a young child, you are malleable and suggestible. This allows you to easily be imprinted with the programming that helps you fit in with the tribe. Ten thousand years ago, if you got kicked out of the tribe, it would mean certain death. That's why biologically we are programmed to experience everything in our tribal setting as the default normal and acceptable way of being. Regardless of whether it's rationally in your best interest or not.

The most unfortunate part about living through something that you perceived as traumatic at a young age is that it gets burned into your subconscious supercomputer mind and you carry it with you every day for the rest of your life as a core wound—unless you go back and change the underlying programming.

Core wounds are the deeply traumatic events that leave a lasting imprint on us, but they are by no means the only way we receive self-limiting subconscious programming. Most of the programming we receive that holds us back is quite subtle and is passed along to us without any malicious intent. Here are some examples of how you might receive self-limiting programming. An obvious one might be your parents' fear around money. Maybe they didn't grow up with a lot of it, and it was hard to come by. By osmosis, they would more than likely pass along the programming to you that you can't be rich and it's hard to make money. Here is another example. If a parent put making money as a priority over the family growing up, you may have resented them for that and subconsciously created an association between money and abandonment. To make sure that pattern doesn't repeat itself, you may take on the programming that as long as I don't make a lot of money, I won't abandon the people I love. Maybe you grew up in a household that said all rich people are assholes. In turn, you would receive the programming that being rich is bad and you shouldn't strive for that unless you want to be an asshole. The subconscious does not think rationally. It just receives inputs through your lived emotional experience and programs you accordingly.

Your programming will ultimately determine the choices you make—for better or for worse. Here are some universal examples of areas in your life that are unquestionably influenced by the programming you received growing up.

- What religion you choose to follow
- What political party you choose to support
- What kind of education you choose to pursue
- What kind of career you choose to pursue
- Who you choose to marry
- What traits you choose to embody as a man or woman

The examples are limitless and oftentimes very nuanced. Personally, I have around thirty-four pages in a Google Doc of pieces of programming that I discovered weren't serving me and that I have had to rewrite in order to unlock a new way of thinking or a new self-empowering habit I wanted to embody.

The saddest thing is that most people will live their whole lives and will never release themselves from the self-limiting programming that they picked up from their tribe, community, or culture. This leads to general resistance toward ways of thinking, talking, and acting that align with the person you have the potential of being. In your daily life, this shows up most often as recurring negative thoughts and bad habits. This was my experience and the experience of every client I have ever worked with. No matter how successful you are, in at least one aspect of life, you will be met with these invisible roadblocks that stem from programming that has placed artificial restrictions on who you have the capacity of being.

BREAKING OUT OF THE MATRIX

If this information is new to you, this should feel like your Neo from the Matrix moment—the awakening to how you were programmed to perceive the world and the corresponding choice that you now need to make in regards to whether you want to continue to be unconscious to all the programming you have received or whether you want to take on the challenge of uncovering what programming may no longer be serving you.

Ultimately, my intentions behind writing this book are (1) introduce you to the fact that in some ways you were programmed to fail (we all were) and (2) share a framework to help you rewrite that self-limiting programming into self-empowering programming that will allow you to fully embrace the potential of who you can be. The truth is that your worst subconscious programming can actually be an incredible gift when you transmute the energy behind it. The same energy that keeps you insecure, low confidence, procrastinating, not showing up fully for yourself and others, and not pursuing your purpose is the same energy that is going to turn you into an absolutely unstoppable force of life.

As the old saying goes, energy cannot be created nor destroyed, so when you do the inner work to reclaim that energy, it will be your greatest propulsion system in life.

We watch motivational videos and read self-help books that tell us to take action, think better thoughts, and be better people, but until the subconscious is in alignment, we will struggle to self-actualize in the world. Acknowledging our self-limiting programming and accepting it for what it is will lead us down the path to reclaim our power.

The beautiful thing about this path is that you don't need to become anything you are not. You just need to remove what is inhibiting you from being who you truly are. You are a sacred being with unique talents. It's your God-given right to give those gifts joyfully. In Part 2 you will get the exact roadmap to do so.

Now that you have an idea of where some of your underlying self-sabotaging programming may be stemming from, let's start down the path of transmuting it.

CHAPTER 2

SELF-AWARENESS AS THE FOUNDATION FOR TRANSFORMATION

The foundation for transformation is awareness. Many of us live our whole lives suffering without even being fully aware of it. We feel uncomfortable and reach for ways to numb the discomfort or distract ourselves but never step into full awareness of the discomfort. Nowadays, there is more discussion around mental health, and many of us have the language to now talk about our feelings. This is a great first step. To grow, we must be aware of where we are starting. Awareness creates the space for transformation, and it all starts with asking ourselves the question in the present moment, *How does it feel to be me right now?* and then feeling the emotions in our body (not our head) without judgment.

Try this out right now for yourself. Instead of thinking about how you feel, try to feel your feelings in your body without attaching a story to them. Simply close your eyes and ask yourself, *How does it feel to be me right now?* Sit with this question—without rationalizing it—until a feeling emerges.

Awareness of how we feel in the present moment is the foundation of the entire human experience. If we aren't fully aware of what it feels like to be us in the present moment, then we have no starting point to work from, which means we have no way to get off the starting blocks.

What I have learned is that the more aware we become, the more we can guide ourselves toward the lives we desire at the deepest level. For example, we live in a highly materialistic world where we are programmed to believe it's the physical things or achievements that will make us happy, but that's not actually true. What we are *actually* after are the feelings we hope those physical things and achievements will produce for us.

We want money to bring us feelings like security, safety, and freedom.

We want the career to bring us feelings like purpose, contribution, and confidence.

We want physical health to bring us feelings like strength, energy, and power.

We want relationships to bring us feelings like love, connection, and being cared for.

Every achievement that we want to unlock tracks back to a feeling we want to experience if we become aware of what is truly driving our behavior. That is why baseline self-awareness is so important and foundational. It allows us to take inventory of what we are doing in our lives right now and how it's making us feel. Furthermore, it allows us to imagine what achievements and experiences may bring us more of our desired feelings in the future. Without being aware of what it's like to be us in the present moment, we lack the perspective to know what will improve our feeling experience in the future.

BEFORE AWARENESS

The year is 2008, I'm eighteen years old, and I just finished my first year playing college football. Well, better put, practicing college football. Although our team had a dismal 1-8 record, I was only able to get on the field during the garbage time of our sole victory that season.

Not only that, but I spent so much time focusing on football (and beer pong) that I finished the semester with a 2.3 GPA. Not good! At this stage in my life, I can honestly say there were three things I really cared about beyond my family and friends: football, girls, and school (in that order). And since I was shitting the bed with both football and school, I was seeking ways to improve myself. Desperately.

Why did football matter so much to me? Simple, my dad wanted me to be an elite basketball player and since that wasn't in the cards for me, football was the next best thing that would get me the affirmation I desired. I was programmed to believe that sport success equaled success in my familial tribe. This was reinforced by the affirmation I received from my social circle growing up.

Why did I care about girls? Well beyond the obvious biological answer, it again came down to my cultural programming. If you grew up in the Western world as I did, you have listened to music, watched movies, and consumed media in our culture that said that as a man, if you're not successful with girls, then you ain't shit. The programming I was running was that the more women I could be sexually intimate with, the more worthy of a human being I would be.

Why did I care about school? I heard it from my parents and every teacher growing up. If you don't graduate from college, you're a failure. I remember one time in high school, my father threatened me with the prospect of having to attend a community college, instead of a four-year university, if I didn't improve my grades. It was very clearly laid out for me that success in school was the only path to success in life. Failing in school meant failing in life. But what specifically did I hope to gain from school?

Thinking back to my senior year in high school, my counselor asked me what I wanted to study in college, and I remember thinking to myself, *I have no fucking clue,* because nothing I had studied in high school seemed remotely interesting enough to want to pursue long-term.

Math class, boring.

Science class, boring.

Foreign language class, boring.

History class, slightly interesting, but how could I make a living memorizing dates of wars from the 1800s?

English class, writing was fun, but I didn't like the books we had to read or the strict structure and style we were forced to follow when writing.

P.E. class, now this was fun! I enjoyed sports, so I decided to pursue college in order to keep playing football.

When applying to colleges and universities, I had to say I was interested in some major, so I said marketing, although I had never taken a marketing class and really had no idea what that meant. All I knew was that Don Draper from *Mad Men* made lots of money, had sex with a lot of beautiful women, and got to travel a lot. Sold! This was a period of my life where most of my decisions were made from a lack of self-awareness. I wasn't conscious of how I felt in the present moment, so I was unable to predict what experiences might make me feel fulfilled in the future. I think a lot of young people and even many adults are living in this same space of unconscious awareness where we see an image of someone projected through social media and think, *Wouldn't that be nice? I don't quite know who I am, but they seem to be happy, so why not try to aim for a life like that person's?*

Additionally, I had no concept of who I was outside of the lens of achievement. It was what I did that made me worth something, and if I wasn't doing anything that could be celebrated, then I wasn't a worthy human being. Keep in mind, I was eighteen years old at the time, so what may seem trivial to an adult feels like the end of the world to a kid with no perspective or life experience.

MY FIRST LESSON IN GAINING AWARENESS

With that being said, my failures in my first semester of football and school sent me on a desperate search to find a way to get my sense of self-worth back, starting with the thing I cared about most: football.

When I went home on winter break, I wandered into my local hole-in-the-wall dingy supplement shop, seeking the magic pill that was going to turn me into a football star. As I walked in the door, I was greeted by a five-foot-six-inch two-hundred-thirty-pound red-haired bodybuilder. Now, this wasn't your normal bodybuilder type. This dude was—different. I had actually been in this shop before—during my senior year in high school—and remembered how he had told me he was finishing his master's degree in neuroscience at the local university.

I found it interesting that he was pursuing studies of the mind while also working in the field of physical fitness. Previously, I would have thought that those two things were mutually exclusive. Everything I had learned in school from ages four to eighteen had led me to believe that if you want to be successful in the "real world," then you need to pick one area of study with a clear linear path to success. Do x, y, and z in this order, and you will be successful. Here was someone blazing an entirely different sort of trail and, as far as I could tell, being fairly successful at it.

As I was quizzing the manager of the shop about what supplements would make me bigger, faster, and stronger, he began turning the questions back on me to find out what I was already doing to enhance my athletic performance. I told him I had been working out hard, following a nutrition protocol to gain muscle, and taking basic supplements like protein, glutamine, a pre-workout, and creatine.

He then asked me if I would be open to trying an exercise that might help me with my performance on the football field. Although I was a hyper-rational kid at the time, I was also very curious. I said, "Sure. Let's try it." He asked me to stand still and look off into the periphery of my eyes for thirty seconds. I thought that was a weird thing to suggest and didn't know how it would help me get more sacks on the football field, but I gave it a shot.

SHHVVOOOOM!! Within thirty seconds, I was transported into a state of calm and relaxation.

It was like I had lived my whole life in the middle of a busy traffic intersection and then whoosh! It's like someone had just come up behind me and gently placed noise-canceling headphones on my ears. The incessant overthinking and negative self-talk that I was burdened with my entire life instantly vanished. The crazy thing was that I didn't even know it was there until it was gone.

At the end of the initial mental exercise, he asked me in his curiously kind yet mischievous way, "How does it feel to be you now?" "I feel calm, and I feel more relaxed," I said.

This may sound crazy, but this was my first memorable experience of stepping into awareness of what it really felt like to be me. Before that, I had nothing to compare my default feeling experience to. Usually, I just felt slightly anxious or super anxious, and getting to experience no anxiety opened up a doorway to infinite possibilities I never even knew existed. Through this subtle experience, I now had the awareness that I could rise above the thoughts in my head and change the way that I felt. Furthermore, I gained the awareness that I had feelings that could be changed. Before that, I was just on an endless roller coaster of highs and lows completely outside of my control. (You will establish your baseline of what it feels like to be you in Part 2, Trainings 1, 3, and 4).

"Now let's try this," he said. "Do the same exercise again, but this time look out the window into the street and describe the cars as they drive by." Initially, I asked him, "How am I supposed to see the cars as they pass by if I am looking off into the periphery?" He encouraged me to try it out and see what happened. Moments later, there I was in this meditative state, looking off into my peripheries but simultaneously still aware of what was happening in front of me.

"A blue car, a green car, a red car," I called out. Behind me, I heard his gentle voice affirm me, "Gooood."

I didn't know it at the time, but he was giving me my first lesson on mindfulness and meditation. He was helping me to awaken my awareness, and I was learning by doing. He intuitively knew I would only "get it" by experiencing it firsthand. Up until then, I had only learned in school by listening to a teacher talk and present material (auditory and visual learning), which is why I think school was so uninteresting for me. I was and am a kinesthetic learner and never got the opportunity to learn that way outside of sports. As I was becoming more self-aware, I was slowly understanding the ways in which I needed to learn to be successful.

The biggest *AHA!* moment in this experience was that I could be aware of and observe the world around me without becoming emotionally attached to it. I could be aware of life events without reacting to them. I could be aware of my thoughts and feelings without needing to identify with them.

Whoa! This was the best drug I had ever tried, and I knew I wanted more.

In a matter of minutes, I felt like I had learned more about myself and how to work with my mind than I had learned in over fifteen years in school. For the first time in my life, I really felt like I had some control over my thoughts and the corresponding feelings that resulted from those thoughts. Immediately, I asked him if he would mentor me in this stuff, and he graciously accepted. I was now officially a student of Sensei Clay.

Fortunately for me, he was way undercharging for the gold he was giving me, so between some help from my parents and the money I had saved from my minimum wage jobs, I was able to go all in with him, training multiple times a week while I was home that winter.

Being an emotionally suppressed kid who had yet to deal with his underlying self-sabotaging programming, I was still living a generally anxious and fearful experience, but I was now at least becoming aware of this.

In psychology, they call this going from unconscious incompetence to conscious incompetence.

I didn't know how my anxiety was being created, but at least I was now aware of it.

Now that I was more aware of my experience, I wanted answers to how this new skill would actually make my life better and help me with priority number one—getting on the football field.

CHAPTER 3
POWER VS. FORCE

OWER BEATS FORCE EVERY TIME. DESPITE all the motivation porn we are fed, success is not a matter of exerting more conscious effort.[2] Effort is a given. The way you create exponential leaps in your performance is by tapping into your power. Your power comes from who you are and not just what you do. Your power is a byproduct of turning off your thinking rational mind, removing the resistance that holds you back at the subconscious level, and allowing yourself to align with the infinite energy source that makes up the entire universe. Many people throughout history refer to this energy as God. Call it whatever makes you comfortable. (We'll explore the exact steps to fully harnessing your power in Part 2.)

Here are some personal examples to show how this plays out in life in the most practical sense. I could force myself to do a boring exercise I hate, like running on the elliptical for an hour where I am constantly checking the time and wishing it would be over already, or I could get completely absorbed into doing a sport I love, like boxing, and burn twice the amount of calories but thoroughly enjoy the process.

Another example of power vs. force is how I go about making a living. For example, I used to have a job scraping paint off fences on a farm. I got paid around $10/hour, and it was back-breaking work I had to force myself to do. Now I get paid over $1,000/hour to coach elite

2   There is a terrific book by David Hawkins that expands upon this concept. The book is called *Power vs. Force*.

33

athletes and business owners to reprogram their subconscious minds, and I love every minute of it. This is possible because I have focused all my energy on harnessing my power. My ability to deliver radical transformations within my clients has nothing to do with my conscious effort and everything to do with my ability to channel my power in the eternal present.

Power comes through subconscious and energetic alignment, combined with maximal effort.

Force comes through conscious effort alone.

Power beats force every time.

Can you reflect on a time in your own life when you were rewarded for harnessing your power instead of forcing things?

LEVERAGING POWER OVER FORCE

Becoming aware of what it was like to be me in that one session with my Sensei was the first step in breaking my rational perception of reality and embracing the power that had been lying dormant inside of me. The fire was lit, and I was ready to carry the torch.

In my first official session with my Sensei, he wanted to show me how I could become more explosive as a defensive end getting off the line of scrimmage. We began with a baseline to see how explosive I was to start. He asked me to jump into the air as high as I could. I did as I was told, and my head was probably six inches or so from the ceiling. Once that baseline was established, he started to guide me through a series of breathing and focusing techniques to gather my energy in a way that he said would allow me to become more explosive.

What I loved about Sensei Clay was that, unlike teachers I had in the past, he had no shame in his game and wasn't trying to convey this aura of superiority over me. He was humble and an expert in toilet zen, which always kept me entertained and engaged with what I was learning. The way he encouraged me to let the energy flow through me was by reminding me how it felt to take a piss. "Bro! Do you squeeze your dick as hard as you can when you're taking a piss?" I laughed. "No." "Well, in that same way, don't try to force the energy. Just let it flow."

So there I was, pulling energy in and breathing like an absolute weirdo, and then he gave me the command to jump up as high as I could. Without thinking, I exploded up and *CRASH* banged my head up against the ceiling! First thought: *Ow!* Second thought: *WTF!? What just happened?*

Immediately, my belief system (my underlying subconscious programming) was spun into chaos as I tried to grasp the fact that I had just jumped six inches higher in the air simply by breathing and visualizing. It didn't fit my current belief system at all. In a matter of minutes, I had increased my vertical leap more than years of training with strength and conditioning coaches. I had always learned that improvement was only about hard work, but I just made a massive improvement and really didn't have to work hard at all. This was my first introduction into this concept of power vs. force. I had just tapped into my power.

Before I had time to try and rationalize how this was possible, he moved me into the next exercise. He took me over to one of those giant see-through refrigerators that housed bottles of ready-made, pre-workout, and protein drinks. This thing probably weighed a solid 300–400 pounds. He instructed me to go along the side of it, get down into my football stance, and explode through the fridge like I would an offensive lineman. I did as I was told and was met with tremendous resistance. I don't think the fridge even moved an inch off the ground. Sensei Clay chuckled and said, "Okay, now do the breathing technique I just taught you and try again." I repeated the breathing and visualization techniques, exploded out of my football stance, and *BOOM!* lifted the fridge two to three feet up off the ground.

"AHHHHH." I felt that adrenaline explode through my veins. I felt like an absolute beast! *Where has this power been all my life?* I thought to myself.

Sensei Clay didn't give my overactive thinking mind time to question what was happening. He taught things in such a matter-of-fact way that it just seemed normal. His belief transformed my belief, and I began to see it as normal as well. Do some deep breathing, visualize some colors and images—and just like that, you make a huge jump in strength and power. Sensei Clay was working his mental alchemy on me as he turned me into a believer in my own power before I had time to overthink it.

I didn't really care how it worked. I just knew it worked and wanted more. Over the next six-week winter break, I got a crash course in what I would now refer to as energy training, and I progressed rapidly—mainly because this was the first time in my life that I actually wanted to do the homework that a teacher had given me.

Learning these techniques and following through with the training on my own was an introduction to how powerful I had the potential of being. I previously believed that more results required more force. Everything I had learned from my parents, teachers, and motivational videos was that if I wanted to be successful, I just had to use more effort. More pushing. More forcing and more doing things I didn't like doing. In the words of Sensei Clay, "You don't need to crush your dick to take a piss, you just have to let it flow." It's not that I wouldn't have to take massive action to get what I wanted. It's that my action could feel like flow instead of force.

Thanks to these new techniques, I was able to set personal records in the weight room and made it onto the football team leaderboard for the first time with a max bench press of 345 pounds. Previously I had only managed a max bench press of 285 pounds. I wasn't trying any harder this time around, but I had found a way to channel more power through these techniques I had learned. For the rest of the school year, I applied the new skills I had learned, using them to get stronger, and I used some of the meditation techniques to counteract stress and anxiety at school.

Fast forward to the end of the school year, and I was finally starting to feel some confidence. My grades improved, and my strength was at an all-time high. I was even having some success with the ladies. There was definitely something to this power-over-force thing, and I was eager to continue to learn more in the coming summer.

CHAPTER 4
BELIEFS SHAPE REALITY

A s we continue on this journey together, I'll be challenging you to think about what you presently believe is impossible for you and how transmuting your self-limiting beliefs (interchangeable with subconscious programming) will expand your possibilities. (We will dive fully into this in Part 2, Training 10.)

This stuff isn't magic. It's just how our subconscious works. Our subconscious has way too much to process in the outside world for us to believe everything is possible. That is why we must be intentional about choosing what we want to believe to be true. Those beliefs filter what we pay attention to and end up driving our behavior long-term. When we choose our beliefs with intention, we step into our power and align ourselves to flow toward the outcomes that we desire most.

YIN AND YANG: BALANCE YOUR ENERGY

Back home for the summer, I was ready to go to the next level with my training. I was already experiencing some success in gains, girls, and grades, and I was eager to see what else my Sensei had in store for me.

Walking back into the dojo (aka my Sensei's dingy old supplement shop), I said, "Yo, Clay! Teach me something new today that will help me dominate on the football field this year." "Well, bud, you already know how to destroy, how about you learn how to heal?" he responded. *Heal?* I thought to myself. *I'm not a doctor. I'm a football player. Why would I need to learn to heal?* Sensei Clay then explained to me how everything in the material universe has both a yin and yang energy and that I would need to master both to unlock my ultimate potential.

The Yang is used to give you energy and is associated with the masculine polarity.

The Yin is used to receive energy and is associated with the feminine polarity.

Although I had, in fact, used yin energy in the past to receive the necessary energy to exert my Yang, up until this point I had not fully recognized the power of yin energy on its own.

As high achievers, we learn that the only way to get to our goal is by using our yang energy. More effort. More force. More trying. This can lead to an imbalance in our energetic system that creates more resistance in our lives and can even lead to physical and emotional harm. When we get into balance by channeling our yin energy, it allows for recharging, alignment, and harmony in the mind, body, and spirit. We must recognize that the energy we are giving must be balanced with the energy we are receiving. Both energies are necessary for any man or woman to become a balanced spiritual warrior.

In the physical training world, this is well established, although not recognized by the terms yin and yang. If you are working out extra hard, you need to balance it with good nutrition, sleep, and recovery modalities. If you don't, the body won't be able to grow, and in the worst-case scenario, you may get injured. Yin and yang both play a role in your journey. Balance your giving with receiving to create harmony and alignment.

At the time, I couldn't fully grasp this concept, but I knew my Sensei had my best interest at heart, so I agreed to spend time working with him to become a healer. One of the first things he taught me about was the energy systems in our bodies. He explained the concept of chakras, which are our main energy centers running down the center of our bodies, and meridians, which are energy highways running throughout the body, delivering energy to every organ and bodily system.

Similarly to the previous winter, I thought this was some woo-woo spiritual B.S. My mom was an atheist, so my default programming was that I was an atheist and anything I couldn't see or couldn't be explained by modern science was not worthy of consideration. I mean, come on, if these energy systems were so important and powerful, why weren't doctors being trained to use them? Why wasn't I taught about them in biology class? Why wasn't this fundamental information taught since the day I was born? Why was this the first time I'd heard the words energy healing, chakras, and meridians? I had never seen or heard of these techniques being used successfully, so I did not believe that it was possible. The rational part of me resisted the idea that this was foundational to my training, but the intuitive part of me, although undertrained, wanted to know more.

One of the first meridians we practiced putting energy into was the governing meridian, which runs from our tailbone, up our spinal cord, up over our head, and ends at our upper lip. He explained that if I opened up the governing meridian by tracing it backward with intentional visualization, I could clear out negative energy, and if I traced it back the other way with healing intention, I could help heal myself and others. Because Sensei Clay talked about these things so matter-of-factly, I, again, took his word for it and suspended my disbelief. I began learning the skills by getting reps in with him tracing these meridians through breathing and visualizing. After an hour or so of practice, I was sent on my way to try it out in the real world.

WHAT YOU ARE SEEKING IS SEEKING YOU

When you start tuning into this energetic world, you begin to realize that there are no accidents or coincidences. Every cause has an effect, and wherever you focus and whatever you choose to do will lead to more of that thing showing up in your life. Since I was so focused on learning this new technique, the universe immediately served me with my first patient. Upon arriving home at my parents' house, I was told that we were going to be joined for lunch by one of my dad's second cousins who I had never met before. When he arrived, I saw that he was a man in his eighties struggling with chronic back pain. Immediately, a light bulb went off in my head, and I thought to myself, *Hmm, I wonder if I can work on his governing meridian and take away his pain.*

Being a naive kid, I said to him, "Hey, how bad does your back hurt?" He then went on to tell me about his years of chronic pain and how it was just something he had accepted at this point in his life. I asked him if I could try and take his pain away. He said, "Sure, why not." I closed my eyes, began breathing deeply, and visualized my way through the exercises I had done at the dojo. I stopped. Opened my eyes. And bullishly told him, "You're healed!" I waited in anticipation for his response. A look of confusion and wonderment crossed his face. He looked at me. Took a few steps around our kitchen. Looked back at me and then proclaimed, "I feel pretty good!" I was exalted! And to be fair, a little bit in disbelief myself. I prodded him with my enthusiasm to share more about what he was feeling. "So are you still in pain?" I asked. "No, I feel good," he responded. *Well, heck yeah!* I thought to myself. *This stuff actually works.*

In that moment of healing, I saw value in yin energy for the first time, and what I believed was possible changed forever.

HOW BELIEFS CREATE YOUR PERCEIVED REALITY

Here is the crazy thing about our beliefs that I will dive deeper into later on. Our beliefs are quite literally our filtration system for what we perceive as our reality.

Let me explain.

At any given moment, we are perceiving reality through our five senses.

We see, hear, smell, taste, and touch the world around us, but those sensory experiences alone have no meaning without a filtration system for them to run through. The filtration system is our subconscious belief system. We will delete, distort, or generalize any information that does not align with what we believe to be true.

For example, let's take running the four-minute mile. Most people have heard the story about how Roger Bannister ran the first four-minute mile. Before that, no one believed it was possible. It was only after this accomplishment was made public, and people were forced to acknowledge that it was possible, that it became possible for all the other runners in the world. Forty-six days after Roger ran a four-minute mile, another person ran it even faster. Then a few more people in the following year. Then a thousand more people in the fifty years following his accomplishment.

Human performance, my performance, your performance is governed by the laws of the universe but also governed by what you believe to be possible for you. My experience with my cousin forced me to change my belief system because I now had evidence for what I previously thought was impossible. I had been inhibiting my potential previously because of the beliefs that I held. Once those beliefs changed, my potential expanded. I now believed it was possible to create healing outside of traditional Western medicine, and my identity was expanded to believe that I could be a healer.

DISEMPOWERING BELIEFS WILL KEEP YOU STUCK

I went on to learn hypnosis, timeline therapy, NLP (neurolinguistic programming), energy work on the meridian and chakra system, and all types of meditation that I saw as useful tools for getting better at football and life. I soaked up all I could, and for the first time in my life, no one had to tell me to study. I would spend hours meditating each day and would try out my healing powers on anyone who would allow me to practice on them. Every positive experience strengthened my new belief system and gave me confidence in my abilities.

As my belief system expanded, I couldn't help but to start to transform internally and externally. Physically I became bigger, faster, and stronger. Mentally I became more resilient, more focused, and more in control of my emotions.

By mid-July, I was flying high, but like many times before in my life, there was a hidden force lurking beneath the surface, ready to bring me back down to reality. One afternoon I was riding my bicycle to my job.

The street I was cruising down was extremely steep. At top speed I hit a small lip in the curb that was a little too big for my flimsy bike to handle, and WOOOSH—over the handlebars and into the air I went. Right before hitting the concrete, I braced myself for impact by extending my arms toward the ground and rolled out of the fall, but not before snapping the radial head of my right arm bone.

I hobbled myself and my busted-up bike to the adjacent post office with tears in my eyes and called my dad to come pick me up. We went to the urgent care, and they confirmed the break with an X-ray. The doctor said I should keep it in a sling and not move it for at least three weeks. *Three weeks?!* I thought. That would almost be the time in which I had to leave for football camp.

Here we go again, I thought. The last time I felt this confident going into a football season was the summer before my junior year in high school when I was getting ready to play on varsity for the first time, and almost the same thing happened to me. I was lifting these old-school steel weights, and my teammate next to me finished a set of military presses with a seventy-five-pound dumbbell and dropped it from about five feet in the air. The weight he dropped fell directly onto my finger, pinning it between another steel dumbbell on the floor that I had just set down. In that moment, my finger was crushed and so were my hopes of getting any serious playing time to start the season. I had to sit out the rest of football camp and the first couple weeks of games, waiting for the broken bone to heal.

Looking back at these events, I could just call this a coincidence, but now I know better. There are no coincidences. There is no bad luck. There are mental laws that govern our universe, and one of those laws is that we will not achieve and/or sustain what we do not believe we are worthy of at the subconscious level. Specifically, my self-limiting subconscious programming was rearing its ugly head again. Did I consciously try to break my finger or arm? No. Was my subconscious going to do anything it could to keep me playing small where I believed I deserved to be? Absolutely. Unfortunately, the subconscious runs the show, and it does things to us and for us without our conscious permission. We see this happen all the time to celebrities who become too successful too fast. Mike Tyson is a great example of someone who believed he deserved to be the world champ, but growing up in poverty, he didn't believe he deserved to be as rich as he was. To put himself back into subconscious alignment, he self-sabotaged and lost tens of millions of dollars just as fast as he had made them. This is very common with athletes who rise to prominence too quickly and get shot down by a barrage of injuries. It is also very common for those who make money too fast in business and end up losing it all shortly thereafter. Your subconscious will do whatever it takes to bring you back into alignment with your beliefs, whether you like it or not.

Reflect personally for a moment.

Have you ever had a big opportunity in front of you—whether it be in your career, financially, in a relationship, or anywhere else—where it all came crumbling down for you right before you were supposed to get your big breakthrough? Every time we shit the bed in a big moment, it's a byproduct of unforeseen self-limiting programming sabotaging you. If this sounds like woo-woo nonsense, think about this. Your subconscious loves stability and homeostasis. Your past way of being and living represents that stability. If you take a big leap into uncharted territory, your subconscious can view this as dangerous and deter you away from it without you ever making the conscious choice to do so.

THE POWER OF OPTIMISM

Despite having terrible subconscious programming, in many ways I always had this flicker of light in my heart that made me believe, for whatever reason, that everything was happening in my best interest. My dad has always been eternally optimistic about the future, and this belief was a gift that I received from him. This bit of programming led to me seeing the diamond in the rough. I had been spending all this time learning how to heal, so this was the perfect case study for me.

Up until that point, my life had been all yang energy. Force it. Work harder. Push harder. My ability to push it with my yang energy was off the table. It was now time to channel that yin energy to heal myself before it was too late. From that moment forward, I did anything and everything to heal my arm ahead of time so that I could get back to training ASAP. With the help of my Sensei, we threw the kitchen sink at it. I walked around with magnets taped to my arm to heal it. I did multiple deep healing meditations every day where I visualized the bone healing together. I did energy training on it, pouring healing energy into the sub chakra where my radial head bone was located. I visualized myself lifting heavy weights to keep my muscles from atrophying. I took Chinese herbs that were supposed to aid the healing process.

I did it all, and it paid off.

Three weeks later, I wasn't just healed, I was repping out 315 pounds on the bench press. I went in to get an X-ray, and it looked like the break had never happened. I had healed myself and had lost minimal strength during the process. This was one of my early *AHA!* moments where I really started to grasp why it was so important to master both yin and yang energy—the ability to step into both my masculine and feminine qualities. Each has its purpose, and each is necessary to become a truly integrated human being.

THE POWER OF BELIEF THROUGH PLACEBO

The truth about my healing process was that nothing I did was new. The power of the mind has been well documented in modern science for years through the power of the placebo. Every year people go through miraculous physical and emotional healing that can only be attributed to the power of belief. In many of these studies, people were told that they were to receive medical intervention but never actually received it. Nonetheless, they miraculously healed—whether it was a placebo pill that healed someone from a disease or a placebo surgery that healed someone's body.

One example of this was a study conducted with 180 participants, looking at the efficacy of arthroscopic knee surgery. This is the most common knee surgery that people receive, and there are over one million knee surgeries every year in the United States alone. What they found in the study was that the placebo produced the same results as the intervention groups over a two-year period. The participants who received the surgery had no better pain relief or function improvement than the placebo group. Furthermore, they found that the placebo group was able to actually outperform one of the groups that received surgery at various points throughout rehabilitation. The power of the mind is fully highlighted in this study and shows just how powerful our belief is as it relates to our ability to heal ourselves.[3]

Another meta-study looking at various research on cardiovascular disease showed significant improvements through taking the placebo pill alone in comparison to medical intervention or the use of pills to improve markers like blood pressure.[4]

3   Alexandra Kirkley et al., "A Controlled Trial of Arthroscopic Surgery for Osteoarthritis of the Knee," *The New England Journal of Medicine* 347, no. 2 (July 11, 2002): 81–88, https://doi.org/10.1056/nejmoa013259.

4   Laura A. Bienenfeld, William H. Frishman, and Stephen P. Glasser, "The Placebo Effect in Cardiovascular Disease," *American Heart Journal* 132, no. 6 (December 1, 1996): 1207–21, https://doi.org/10.1016/s0002-8703(96)90465-2.

Yet another meta-study looking at health outcomes for Parkinson's disease showed the efficacy of the placebo versus other medical interventions. This was due to an increase in dopamine in the brain from the anticipation of receiving a pill they believed would improve their symptoms. This again points to how the participants were able to heal themselves through the power of belief alone.[5]

An example of our ability to heal ourselves from mental disease can be found in a study that was conducted on participants who were suffering from depression. The results in the less severely depressed participants who took a placebo pill were often indistinguishable from the response rate to antidepressant pills. This shows again the power we hold to heal ourselves and change the way we feel.[6]

Open up Google Scholar and search "placebo." You will find countless studies that show how the power of belief can perform as well or even better than medical intervention. Instinctively we know we have the power to heal ourselves, but very few of us are taught how, so we don't believe it's possible. Through my lived experiences, my belief system was now expanding, and I knew I was capable of what I previously perceived as supernatural.

With two weeks to go before football camp started, it was time to put this new belief in myself to the test.

---

5   Raúl De La Fuente-Fernández and A. Jon Stoessl, "The Placebo Effect in Parkinson's Disease," *Trends in Neurosciences* 25, no. 6 (June 1, 2002): 302–6, https://doi.org/10.1016/s0166-2236(02)02181-1.

6   Walter A. Brown, "Placebo as a Treatment for Depression," *Neuropsychopharmacology* 10, no. 4 (July 1, 1994): 265–69, https://doi.org/10.1038/npp.1994.53.

CHAPTER 5
FINDING YOUR UNIQUE TALENT

O UR UNIQUE TALENT IS SOMETHING THAT is revealed through exploring our curiosities. Our unique talent is the intersection between what we are good at, what we enjoy most, and what can contribute to something greater than ourselves. Healing other people was that for me. This was the first time in my life that there was something I enjoyed—something that actually came easy to me—that made other people's lives better.

Can you think about where that intersection is for you? The more you can align with your unique talent, the more powerful you become. (If you don't already know what it is, you'll be able to discover your unique talent in Part 2, Training 7.)

PUTTING MY MENTAL SKILLS TO THE TEST

I packed my bags and started the thirteen-hour drive back to college for pre-season football camp. I was feeling confident and ready to dominate my competition. Needless to say, at this point, I was dancing to the beat of my own drummer. I knew I had stumbled upon something I was passionate about but still had nothing else definitive to channel my energy into besides football. That would soon change. I had a chip on my shoulder going into camp because I knew the way I was going about my training was rubbing some of my coaches the wrong way. In one team weightlifting session, I was doing some deep breathing techniques to conjure my energy and visualize the weight I was about to lift when I heard my head coach yell, "What the fuck is Epstein doing?!" I ignored him, took my weight off the rack, and busted out my set of heavy squats. I knew I was onto something and wasn't about to let his judgment deter me from using my new mental skills. The subtle way the coaches told me they thought I was a joke was by giving me the number 69 for my jersey, signaling I was the jester on the team.

The funny thing is that at the time, there was legit peer-reviewed scientific research that showed the efficacy of visualization for increased strength, so what I was doing was not even outside the realms of mainstream science.[7] It was just outside of the set of tools we were being taught on our football team.Anything outside of the status quo in any subculture will often be met with resistance. This resistance stems from a collective subconscious field that holds people in a select paradigm that is attached to the members' identities. No one likes to have their identity challenged, because it creates instability in the self. That instability triggers fear even if the new paradigm could actually be in their best interest to adopt. This is part of what keeps many disciplines and tribes stuck and stagnant. They are afraid to let go of what *was* to embrace what *could be*. In many ways, that is the journey we are on together here. We are questioning the subconscious programming that we hold in all aspects of life and challenging ourselves to adopt a new identity that represents more possibilities.

7   One study that affirmed what I was doing with these mental tools was conducted on three groups of college students where the goal was to make them stronger at the bicep curl exercise over the course of six weeks. This study split the students into three groups. The first group just did the bicep exercise alone. The second group visualized doing the bicep exercise but never touched the physical weights. The third group did both the visualization and the physical exercise. The results were as you may expect. The third group that visualized and did the exercise far outperformed the other two groups. What's crazy, though, is that the other two groups performed exactly the same!—meaning, the group that didn't touch the weights, but did the mental reps, got the same results as the group that was actually lifting the weights every week. That study always stuck with me, because it appeased the rational part of my mind that felt like I needed to prove something to those around me who thought I was just being a weirdo with my visualization techniques. https://www.tandfonline.com/doi/abs/10.1080/1612197X.2009.9671890.

Soon I had my first opportunity on the football field to flex my new mental muscles. We would do drills where we'd line up as defensive linemen against the offensive linemen and try to get past them in order to get the quarterback. This was some straight-up gladiator shit. Testosterone through the roof. Man vs. man. Pure violence.

I could hear Tupac's "California Love" playing over the speakers as we started the drill, and my teammates were yelling and hollering like a pack of wild animals. I got down into my football stance and was lined up against a senior on the team who weighed at least sixty to seventy pounds more than I did. I didn't care. I knew I would dominate him. I hit a technique my Sensei taught me called the iron shield, where I pulled energy in through my root and crown chakras and felt my body electrify with intensity and power. Coach snapped the ball, and I bulldozed through the best offensive lineman on our team like it was nothing. I got him off balance and went right to the quarterback.

"Wooooo!!" I screamed. I had arrived. I thought to myself, *I'm not going to lose any of these one-on-ones for the rest of camp.* I was beginning to reprogram myself to believe that no one could beat me. Unbeknownst to me at the time, there are two ways to program yourself and change your belief system:

1. Through positive experiences that are repeated enough to create a new belief.
   This is how I was forming self-belief at the time. I was proving to myself in real-time through my success that I was capable.

2. Through a technique that requires no physical experience that I would discover a decade later.

Stick with me. I will teach you that second technique later, because it's much more effective. But first, we have to go on this journey together so you can see how I got there.

Although I was learning many deeply energetic and spiritual techniques, there were still many gaps in my subconscious programming that were limiting my conscious evolution and leading to my physical breakdown. Emotionally, I was flying high from my early success at camp as I stepped into this new identity that encompassed a belief in my ability to perform at the college level, but simultaneously my body was starting to break down physically. The best explanation I have for what was happening is that I had this insane airplane engine trying to power a tiny Fiat. I was also getting burned up from the inside out because I was expending far too much energy in comparison to how much I was able to regenerate.

The health and strength of my own body continued to deteriorate as the first week of the football season approached. I needed to wrap my ankles and take a handful of ibuprofen just to be able to run during practice. In our first game, I had achieved what I had been training for since the end of the previous season. I was the starting defensive end. No longer relegated to the bench. I was in the game. When the season finally started, I was physically half the man I was, coming into football camp, but I didn't let that stop me from having some breakout performances. In one game, in particular, I was named defensive player of the game with a sack, a couple of QB hurries, a couple of tackles for loss, and five tackles overall. In this game, I experienced one of my first pure states of flow where, despite battling injuries, I elevated my performance beyond anything I'd experienced before.

I can feel it now. I was like a horse with blinders. No thinking. Just being. Just performing. Just allowing all the subconscious programming aligned with being a badass defensive end to take over. When the ball was snapped, my body knew what to do and guided me to be in the right position at the right time to make the right play. This was pure flow, and it opened my mind up to what's possible when I let go of control.

Flow is an experience we've all had before and is the optimal state of being that any of us want to be in when we are performing our craft. We get to experience flow when we have already built the conscious skills necessary to perform an action without thinking and can surrender to our subconscious programming that has already been wired through hundreds, if not thousands, of previous repetitions. Once you have that skill built, it's just a matter of letting go of control so you can allow yourself to embrace the skills you already have.

By the end of the season, I was so bruised up that I was using crutches to get around to class during the day and then using excessive ibuprofen to get through practice and games at night. I kept pushing through and had another outstanding game with thirteen tackles, but ultimately as a team, we finished the season with a 3-6 record, and I finished with a broken body. Football-wise, I felt like I had proven everything to myself that I wanted to prove. I proved to myself I could be a starter for a college football team and that I could be dominant when healthy.

STEPPING INTO MY UNIQUE TALENT

During this same time frame, as I enjoyed the results of my training on the football field, I discovered my unique talent: my ability to heal others and help them step into their greatest potential. This was something beyond football, girls, and school—something of my own. I remember one night in particular my super anxious friend and teammate had this severe migraine that had him on the verge of tears. I thought to myself, *I've never tried, but I'm sure I can heal that.* I took him into a dark dorm room, led him through a guided meditation to release the pressure he was putting on himself, did some energy healing on him to put him into a relaxed state, and—just like that!—he was healed. All the pain was gone, and a huge grateful smile washed over his face. This triggered a deep feeling of pride and purpose within me and was really one of the first times where I thought that this might be the reason I was put on this earth. (I'll walk you through how to find your unique talent in Part 2, Training 7.)

This was one of the first times I received external validation from my friends for something that was truly aligned with my unique talents. As I'm sure you've experienced before, one of the best feelings you can have is one of being of service. It's baked into our biology to make us feel good when we help people that we care about. This was a catalyst for wanting to share more of my gift with my teammates, friends, and people I cared about.

Eventually, word got around that I had some unusual ability to heal people, and so my teammates started coming to me before practice to take their pain away. Alongside the athletic training staff, I would support my fellow teammates the best I could before practice to help relieve their pain. I was named the Guru by the athletic trainer working with the team, which probably wasn't the best thing for my nineteen-year-old ego, but hey, I was figuring out this new identity. We had a one-two punch where she would give them the Western medicine, and I would apply the Eastern medicine—a.k.a. my magic.

I was now entering a new season of life where I had identified my unique talent to physically and emotionally heal people, and that is what I wanted to pour all my energy into. To create space for my own healing journey, I stepped back from my football career and began my journey as a healer and coach.

CHAPTER 6
THE THIRD PATH

T
HERE IS ALWAYS A THIRD PATH when you have the courage and
patience to seek it out. Is there an area in your life where you feel
like you're stuck between a rock and a hard place? Many times in life
we will be faced with a situation where our options will seem binary. It
will feel like we are at a fork in the road. Do I put my family first or my
career? Do I get more work done, or do I make time to work out? We
will constantly be put in these situations in life where it will seem like
we have to give up something we really want and settle for some safer
but less desirable option. This does not need to be true.

In my experience and through dozens of client case studies, I have
seen that you can forge a new path forward when you open yourself
up to a new paradigm of being. Challenge yourself to seek out a third
path. Even if that means you are taking the road less traveled or paving
your own path forward. This may require that you call into question old
limiting beliefs, and that's the point. You may not be able to create the
third path until you transcend your self-perceived limitations. It will
require going out of your comfort zone, but the reward is that you will
design a life you truly want to live (Part 2 will set you up mentally to
discover the third path when you need it).

FINDING THE THIRD PATH
After the football season ended, I shifted my focus back to how I was
going to harness my unique talent to pursue an education and hopefully

a career. By the time winter rolled around, I was receiving pressure from my professors to pick a major. Similarly to high school, I still had not taken any classes in college that sparked enough interest within me to want to pursue a specific major. I knew what I wanted to study, but it didn't align with any of the college majors available at my school. It was clear to me that whatever major I chose needed to be actionable and contribute to this career path I saw myself going down. I felt a little lost about what my next step would be, but I had this intuition that a third path would emerge if I continued seeking it. A third path is the emergence of a course of action outside of what previously was perceived as a binary decision. This happens all the time in life where the two choices both feel not right, and you are forced to sit into the tension of that until a third path emerges. An example might be in your job where you want to quit, and it seems like there are only two options. Stay or leave. The third path might be to stay on as a consultant, where you do what you are best at, while cutting out the responsibilities that made you want to quit in the first place. The third path is never the comfortable path, because it requires that you look deeply within yourself, but it is always the right path, because it gets you where you need to be.

Before long, I heard about my college's scholars program. Apparently, some students at my school could design their own major if they were willing to defend it in front of a panel of professors in the corresponding educational departments. This immediately felt like me. An opportunity to dance to a beat that I was drumming and own the educational path I would be pursuing. I was super stoked about this opportunity and went in to meet with the head professor of the kinesiology department to share the idea I had for a self-designed major I was calling "The Mental Aspect of Human Performance."

I wanted to take my love for the mind and body connection and create a concrete skillset I could use when I graduated school. This professor and her wife (also head of the department) were not the biggest fans of mine. Not knowing anything about who I was outside of my role on the football team, I got the label of meathead white male athlete looking to exploit his privilege to get away with breaking the rules and getting an easy path to a degree. I remember she straight up said to me, "I don't think you have the discipline or intelligence to design and execute this type of major."

Bet!

That's all I had to hear. I've always had this underdog mentality about me, and when I had a nemesis in these department heads to fight against, my fire was lit. In the same way that I wanted to prove my football coaches wrong, I now wanted to prove these professors wrong. This definitely wasn't the most conscious way to go about this, but it was perfect for the level of consciousness I was at in this moment. Despite being met by resistance by a couple of these professors, I ended up finding a couple other professors who were willing to support and believe in my vision. They sponsored my request to join the scholars program, and with their help, I eventually designed my major and had the opportunity to defend it in front of the department heads.

PERFORMANCE ANXIETY

At this point in my life I had no experience with public speaking, and the thought of speaking in front of a panel that was going to judge me was terrifying. See the pattern here? High pressure leads to high anxiety, which leads to that same *I'm worthless, I'm not enough* hidden programming bubbling up to the conscious surface.

As previously mentioned, the path to removing that self-limiting programming starts with awareness, so as you read this, if you can remember times in your life where you sabotaged yourself, write it down and ask yourself what you were focusing on in the moments leading up to that poor performance. Were you overthinking or just letting yourself embrace the present moment?

At the time, my self-limiting programming that was driving my poor public speaking performance was hidden to me, so I just thought I was bad at public speaking. When spring rolled around, it was finally time for the rubber to meet the road. I had to give a presentation where I needed to convince a panel of professors that I was worthy of pursuing my self-designed degree. I was prepared to present my degree on paper, but mentally I was not equipped with the skills to give a good performance.

As soon as I got on stage, I turned red in the face and started sweating profusely. I was wearing a suit and had already sweat all the way through my dress shirt by the time I had to present. It was high school history class all over again. I stumbled my way through the presentation red as a beet, sweating my balls off and feeling completely chaotic within my own head. I really wasn't sure if I was going to get in, but at least I had all my ducks in a row and had done the work necessary to receive entrance into the program. Despite giving a poor performance, I had busted my ass with the logistical part of designing my degree, and I had done just enough to get by.

A few weeks later, I received a letter from the scholars program in my school mailbox.

ACCEPTANCE.

I had received permission to follow my self-designed path toward an education of my choosing.

CHAPTER 7

STEPPING INTO A NEW IDENTITY

MANY OF US LIVE OUR WHOLE lives believing that we are relegated to a certain identity. I'm fat. I'm poor. I'm depressed. I'm dumb. I'm not lovable. I'm not charismatic. Each one of those identities is just a byproduct of self-limiting beliefs that can be changed.

If you want to step into a new reality, it starts with letting go of your old self-limiting identity. When you remove negative thought patterns and habits, what remains is the true you. A version of you that is in alignment with your highest self in the area of your life that you chose to focus on. During the events portrayed in this chapter, I transcended the version of myself that believed I would always be poor and over-weight. As I released that old identity, I was left with an identity that was aligned with who I truly am. Can you think of an old identity that you need to let go of so you can step into who you truly are?

BREAKING THROUGH THE OLD IDENTITY

As I began the path to pursue my studies in the mental aspect of human performance, I was once again disappointed by the educational system. I took classes about the body, where I studied exercise physiology, nutrition, biomechanics, and anatomy. I took classes about the mind, where I studied psychology, the history of rituals in sports, neuroscience, and sport psychology. Despite taking the most relevant classes available at my university, nothing could compare to the lessons I was receiving from my Sensei and from books I was reading outside of the university setting. I was looking for an application of what was being taught in the classroom. Real-world skills. Things I could do and use to feel and perform better. I kept waiting for a class that was going to teach me how I could manage my emotional state or improve my physical performance in the real world. Nothing. Everything was about theory, and nothing was relevant to real-world application.

You may be thinking that's what advanced degrees are for, but my view of it was that if I wasn't getting value in these four years of school, it would be insane to go back into this same education system, hoping to get a different result. My parents and I had already invested tens of thousands of dollars into getting a bachelor's degree, and I was going to walk away from it learning less practical information than I had learned spending hundreds of dollars and weeks training with my Sensei.

What became obvious was that if I wanted to build on what I had learned from my Sensei, I needed to look outside of the classroom. It was then that I started to have my awakening that school wasn't the be-all end-all path to success that my teachers and parents had told me it would be. Despite being let down by the opportunities for growth in my current educational experience, I was determined to find a way to get something valuable from the limited time I had left.

It so happened that I had to complete my senior project to graduate. I decided to use the techniques that helped me with football to pursue my first bodybuilding competition. I would utilize all the tactics I'd learned so far to get myself ready to compete in this competition and would document the process as a case study, which would serve as the centerpiece for my senior project.

The bodybuilding thing was a unique challenge because I had to drop enough body fat to reveal six-pack abs for the first time in my life. I was around 240 pounds with about forty pounds of body fat that I needed to lose. At twenty-one years old, this, again, was a major milestone for me as I went through my personal evolution. Previously, I never thought it was possible to get that lean and actually have a six pack, so I needed to take the steps necessary to break through that old identity so that a new one could emerge.

Since I didn't yet have the subconscious reprogramming techniques I now have at my disposal, I had to get this done through pure force and will. (Luckily for you, I will walk you through an easier way to accomplish this in Part 2, Trainings 8 and 9.) I was training harder than ever before and eating more strictly than ever before. Nothing was new about these physical techniques, but it was the consistency, which challenged me mentally. The consistency to not fall into my old habits and the consistency to follow through with my new habits. Every night before I went to bed and every day when I was doing my cardio, I was setting a subconscious GPS destination to work toward. I visualized what I would look and feel like if I had a six pack and imagined myself living in that 3D reality as if it was my present reality. While all my college friends drank beer, ate pizza, and partied, I stuck to the regimen. I had a singular focus. Get shredded. Do whatever it takes to get shredded.

Along the way, I would feel the doubts creep in and wonder why I was sacrificing so much for doing a bodybuilding show when I had no desire to actually be a bodybuilder. In the toughest moments, I would go into meditation and progressively relax my body until my cravings, anxiety, and self-doubt melted away.

Going into the show, I weighed in at 197 pounds and, for the first time in my life, had six-pack abs. I had officially transcended the version of myself that believed it was impossible for me to get that lean. I competed in the show, did not win, but had the time of my life flexing to the song "Hallelujah" on stage while I basked in my six months of hard work.

Since that day, I've had six-pack abs and have never looked back. The crazy thing is that the previous identity that I held believed that six-pack abs were one of those impossible feats that only people on

TV or in magazines could attain. Once my identity shifted, I was now programmed to view this as my new default way of being. It became very matter-of-fact. Sometimes when people manifest things like this, they point to the law of attraction, but I actually think that discounts the hard work that I put in. The physical habits laid the blueprint, and my mental habits are what allowed me to sustain that blueprint all the way through to the finish line. By the end of the competition, I knew that this was the new me. I was a shredded dude. It was my identity, and it will be until the day I die.

LEARN. APPLY. TEACH.

Now I knew that the techniques I had learned had real-world applications and worked for me. But I wanted to learn more. How could I use them to help others? One day the universe delivered for me. I saw an email come through my inbox about an educational grant that was available for students who had an idea they wanted to explore through research. My success with my senior project triggered an idea for me to apply the visualization techniques I had been using to get stronger in the weight room to a real-life research study. I decided that I would try to run a study of male college students who wanted to do the two things I cared most about at the time: lifting heavier weights and feeling less stress/anxiety.

I applied for the research grant, and a couple of months later, I was approved.

It was surprisingly easy to get this research grant where they would be giving me $7,500 to conduct this study without any major oversight or accountability. The big takeaway for me was that someone would give me money doing something I loved. This was the most money I've ever had in my life, which was a game changer. Previously, I had only worked minimum-wage jobs, and my bank account was constantly hovering between $0–$300. Yes, I had to use some of that money to conduct the study, so it wasn't all going to be cash in my pocket, but I at least had a foundation to start from.

This was the first time I could actually breathe a little bit—thanks to my pursuit of cultivating my unique talent. Usually you hear the more straight-edged realistic people of the world say that following your passion is a good way to go broke, but this experience in itself was planting the seed of belief within me that I could make a living doing what I loved.

A big point I want to make here is that my passion for this field of study was in no way contrived. It was all a natural byproduct of pursuing my curiosities. I wasn't rationally thinking about how I could make the most money possible. I was being pulled in a direction that started with a genuine desire to get better at football, and it was leading me down a path to a potential career in mental performance coaching.

When the study finally started, I had six weeks to get these dudes stronger and significantly less stressed. Half of the students were in my control group, where they did no mental training, and the other half were in my experimental group, where they would go through my visualization meditation techniques with me each week before performing the bench press exercise. Not surprisingly, my experimental group kicked ass. They showed significant strength improvement compared to the control group and had proven to me and to themselves that doing these techniques would make them stronger. Furthermore, this was the experimental group's first exposure to meditation, and the practice helped them manage stress at school in a way that they never before experienced. The strength gains were cool, but the tool for reducing stress was one that they could carry with them for the rest of their lives.

This was my first *AHA!* moment that it wasn't just me that could get stronger and feel less stressed doing these meditation techniques. Other people had the same benefits as I did, and it opened my mind to a whole new world of possibilities. I now knew I had what it took to create real-world results. By the end of my senior year, I was ready to leave the amateurs behind and go pro with my mental performance skills.

CHAPTER 8

WHAT WE CAN'T ACCEPT WON'T CHANGE

CCEPTING SHORT-TERM FAILURE CAN FEEL LIKE a major challenge, but once it is accepted, it opens up the door to new possibilities. Acceptance of reality as it is instead of how you wish it would be is the first step in getting yourself out of a bad situation. As one of my favorite zen proverbs goes, "What we can't accept won't change." Accept your situation for what it is, and you will have the power to change it. The same goes for the beliefs that we hold. We must first accept that we hold a disempowering belief before we gain the ability to release it and replace it with something that empowers us. Think about acceptance as the second step after awareness. Once you become aware of something you don't like, you can still suppress it and compartmentalize it. The only way you can actually change it is by fully accepting it as it is. This releases the energy and frees you up to let it go into the past and take a new course of action in the present.

EXPLORING POSSIBILITIES

Upon graduation, I needed to identify the next step on my journey toward going pro as a mental performance coach. I knew I wanted to do something outside of the box that utilized my unique skills, but I had no idea how I would actually make a full-time living. I had never met a mental performance coach in real life and had no clear path to success—let alone a place to get started. On my way back home, I carpooled with my buddy from high school who was a bit of a business savant and had already started his career as an entrepreneur. He had started a mobile app company at eighteen years old and was raking in enough money to live off of already. This fascinated me because I had never met an entrepreneur before and didn't even really see starting my own business as a viable option. My buddy had also just finished playing Division 1 basketball at a neighboring university in Los Angeles. During our thirteen-hour drive together, we talked non-stop about the power of the mind and how it could be used to enhance performance. Throughout his college career, he was never given these mental tools to enhance his performance, so he was eager to learn more.

When we got back to our hometown, I started to train him in my mental techniques, and as he started to become a more dominant basketball player, he had an *AHA!* moment. "Dude, these meditations should be apps!" he told me after one of our sessions. I had zero idea how to start a business, let alone a mobile application business. I told him about my concerns, but he encouraged me to take the leap with his guidance. With his expertise and the few thousand dollars I had left over from my research grant, we started a mobile app company teaching these meditation techniques. This was back in 2012 when the app store was still in its infancy, and within a few months of launching our first app, we started to actually make some sales. People were really buying my meditation app and using it to get better. Another pathway to success opened in my mind.

By the following summer, I decided to take my talents to a bigger market to see if I could expand my mind and possibilities. My friend-business partner and I moved to Austin, Texas, and got to work. Within eighteen months, we produced sixty-nine mobile apps in the wellness space by following a strategy called app reskinning. Essentially, we would take the same app code from the previous app and then add a new design with new content to create a completely new app we could submit to the app store. I made meditation apps for everything from sleeping better to playing better basketball to relieving anxiety to overcoming addiction and just about every other category I could think of. This reskinning concept initially seemed like a great idea to get my meditations to more people.

Before long, we were making around $4,000 a month, and I assumed the business would just keep scaling. I assumed wrong. Despite making more and more apps, our downloads plateaued, and so did our revenue. Since we were 50/50 partners, I was getting into a pretty precarious position trying to live on $2,000 a month while paying $1,600 a month on rent alone. Nonetheless, I had the hope that we would break through this plateau. I charged the expenses I didn't have the cash for and kept pressing forward.

By this time, I had transitioned out of my creative, passionate zone of genius (making meditations) and was spending all my time doing operational tasks to try and get more downloads on our apps. Instead of using my unique talents, I was now essentially an operations manager at my company. As the company continued to plateau, I felt more and more dissatisfied with the path I was now on. What started as a passion project now felt like a prison. I was working day and night to get these apps into the world and gave up working with the few one-on-one clients I had altogether to make this business work. By the end of my second year in Austin, I was completely broke both financially and spiritually.

This was a particularly difficult part of my journey, where all my self-limiting money beliefs were being pressed to the surface for me to examine. I felt like I could really help people with the skills I had gained, but the money just wasn't showing up for me. I was getting into more and more debt by attending money-making workshops, hiring coaches to help me make money, and investing in courses I thought would help me make money. Nothing was working, and every trip to the grocery store where I had to pull out my credit card was a reminder.

Every time my card was swiped, it felt like a knife being twisted in my gut. My subconscious was still running the programming that money correlated with my self-worth, and this sent me down a deep shame spiral. Even though I was making lots of friends in this new city, I was always being followed around by this dark cloud—lack of money—that didn't fully allow me to enjoy the present moment.

One bright spot during this time was meeting in an elevator a dude who I instantly hit it off with (this will be important later). He was a guy like me who had played college football, but instead of going into entrepreneurship, he had gone into corporate software sales. Funny enough, he was financially abundant but was seeking more of what I had been investing in the previous six years. He wanted to go deeper into his own personal growth and fulfillment by starting a company he was passionate about.

I started coaching him in the meditation techniques I had, and he experienced instant results. He felt empowered and confident to pursue a path aligned with his unique talents. Our coaching relationship turned into a friendship, and we joined forces to start running free group workouts for our friends where he would lead the exercises, and afterward I would lead a cool-down yoga and meditation session. Although we weren't getting paid any money to run these workouts, I felt my passion ignited. I was helping people while using my unique talents, which gave me a euphoric feeling.

Unfortunately, by this time I was already so far into credit card debt that I could no longer afford to live in my apartment and was forced to leave this budding community and our weekly rooftop workouts in my rearview mirror.

MENTAL RESET

What we can't accept won't change. It took me a relatively long time to accept that my app company was not going to be what I had hoped. It seemed like the perfect opportunity, but the company struggled to grow, and my credit card debt piled up. I had to accept my failure and move forward. I made the decision to hit the reset button on my life once again. Some new internet friends of mine had recently moved down to Medellin, Colombia, and were singing the praises of how good the lifestyle was there.

Beautiful weather, beautiful women, and an overhead of less than $1,000/month. Sold.

Out of pure necessity, I almost immediately got rid of everything I had aside from two suitcases, sublet my apartment, and prepared to move down to Medellin without any idea of what the future had in store for me. Before I left, I worked with a bankruptcy company to help me consolidate my debt, so I could start to pay it off and get myself back on track again. The only problem was that I was making around $2K/month, and my debt payment alone was $1K/month. I needed some fast cash to start this process of getting out of debt. To do so, I pleaded with my business partner to sell the company with me. However, being a savvy businessman, he saw this company making around $60K/year as the perfect passive income stream to continue feeding money into his pocket without any effort. He refused to sell the company but offered to buy me out for $20,000.

This was devastating for me. The content in these apps was my life's work up until this point, and after some conversations with potential buyers, I knew that if we sold this company, we could make at least $100K. Nonetheless, I was out of options.

Have you ever felt like your back was against the wall where you had to accept short-term pain to set yourself up for long-term success? This is a natural part of the process when we strive for more in life. The pain that feels like a door closing is always followed by the relief of another door opening if we can maintain focus and optimism.

I knew that the path I was on was not sustainable. I was running a company no longer in alignment with who I wanted to be and no longer sustainable if I wanted to make a living. I accepted my failures and decided I would use them as a learning experience to launch off into the next chapter of my life. It was an excruciating experience to wipe the slate clean in regard to all the work I had put in, but I took the deal—pocketed the $20K ($5K/month over four months) and moved down to Medellin, Colombia, to start over again.

CHAPTER 9

THE POWER OF SURRENDER

Surrender is a skill that allows you to let go of what is not in your control. So often we trap ourselves in a state of regret and stagnation by mulling over past events that we cannot change or future pacing worries that haven't yet happened. Surrender is a skill that you can strengthen with practice. Whenever you catch yourself thinking about something outside of your control in the present moment, take a deep breath, acknowledge it for what it is, and then bring yourself back into the eternal now by asking yourself, *What can I do or focus on right now that will propel me toward where I want to be?* Additionally, sometimes the answer is to do nothing and just allow yourself to sit in the tension of what's happening in the moment. Life is always happening right now, and the more you can surrender to what's happening now, the better you will feel and the more capable you will be to take action.

FACING REALITY

Upon arriving in Colombia, I was met with the repercussions of my decision immediately. I spoke no Spanish (outside of hola, baño, and como estas), and now that I had sold my only income stream, I had to figure things out quickly before my limited runway ran out. About a month after arriving, I had yet to get any traction doing my client work and was reaching my breaking point emotionally. Before then, I had just put my head down and powered forward with optimism, but the losses were stacking up and I was losing hope. One day after looking over my finances and lack of opportunities in front of me, I finally broke down in a fit of frustration. I sat on the bed in my 100 sq. foot room, cried my eyes out, and was ready to give up on my dream.

My self-sabotaging subconscious programming burst through louder than ever before, hurling insults at me in my own head.

"How could you be so stupid?!"

"Who did you think you were, trying to start a company?"

"You'll never make money doing what you love!"

"You're not good enough to be a full-time mental performance coach."

"Just give up and get a normal job with some stability."

The voice in my head lambasted me with meaner things than my worst enemy would ever say to me. The subconscious mind is great at that, because it knows all your deepest insecurities. I went onto the roof of my apartment, looking over this beautiful new city I was living in, and remembered what my Sensei had taught me. He was and is the ultimate survivor. He always said to approach problems with this question: *If I could do it, how would I do it?*

So, for my situation, "If I could make enough money to make a living, how would I do it?"

"If there was a way for me to make it out of this, how would I start?"

After I fully surrendered the past and accepted the cards I was now dealt, I could start to move forward. A lot of people have a misconception about what it means to surrender. Surrendering in this context is not the same as giving up. When you surrender your past circumstances, it actually creates space for a new and better reality to emerge in the present. Until you let go of what was, you will not have the space to step into what can be. Once I did this, the eternal optimist in me finally broke through and got me back into brainstorming mode. I took out a notepad and started free-flowing every potential solution that came to mind, no matter how silly it seemed to my rational mind. One of my favorite gems that I learned from Sensei Clay was that the second you say the words "I don't know," your subconscious shuts down its ability to find an answer for you.

To this day, I refuse to say, "I don't know." If I don't have the answer, I say, "I am seeking solutions." That way I keep the door open for my subconscious to bubble up a next step for me when the time is right. One thing we forget about our subconscious mind is that it has stored impressions from millions and millions of experiences and memories in our lives. Unlike the conscious mind, it has the ability to think nonlinearly and will provide you with potential solutions that your conscious mind would never think of. It can only do this when you fully surrender to it, though, and trust that the solutions will in fact reveal themselves to you if you stay diligent.

The reason we don't want to just rely on our conscious mind is because it doesn't allow us to dig deeper into the depth of knowledge and experience that is available in our subconscious supercomputer mind. Your subconscious has the processing power to provide you with breakthrough solutions.

The next time you feel stuck in any aspect of your life, put on some binaural beats from YouTube, close your eyes, and sit with yourself for half an hour, asking questions like:

If I could find a solution to my problem, how would I do it?

If there was a first step to getting to a solution, what would it be?

After I had purged everything that had bubbled up from my brain onto my brainstorming list, I took a deep breath and paused. I saw one intersection on that list that made the most sense to me. It was the intersection between "cash and my passion." (You will experience the creation of your own lists in Part 2, Training 7.) Although there were a million businesses I could try and start to make money, I knew I would not be able to sustain them, because they were not aligned with my unique talents. What was aligned was my burning desire to help others through my one-on-one client work. I understood that it might take years to build this business, but it would be worth it, because I would never give up on it.

TOOLS FOR MOVING FORWARD

With a new goal to work toward, I dove back into working on my own personal growth to keep me in an empowering state of mind during this challenging time. There are a few tools I used to keep my mind clear during this emotionally charged time. The first was journaling. A couple of years back, I had interviewed one of the leading psychologists who studied journaling, and he told me journaling was only scientifically proven to be good for two things:

1. Catharsis: To purge all the negative thoughts and stories in your head so they felt heard and no longer needed to circulate within your head.

2. Creativity: To free flow ideas in a way that gets them out of your head so they can take form on paper.

I made journaling almost a daily practice for those two reasons. Mainly the first, though. Funny thing is that nowadays I almost never journal. Maybe once every month or two I'll have something come up that I want to purge onto a piece of paper. As we will dig into later, this can be directly attributed to the work I did to clean up my inner planet (Part 2, Training 10). Another thing I did to keep me focused was write out the clear outcomes I wanted for my life. (You will do this in Part 2, Trainings 8 and 9.) I scripted a vision of how much money I wanted to make, what kind of relationship I wanted to be in, what kind of health I wanted to have, and how I wanted to feel. I didn't have any of those outcomes at the time besides good health, but at least I knew where I was going. I read these outcomes every day to constantly bring my subconscious mind back to my ideal vision for my life. If an action did not align with getting those outcomes, I would not give it my energy. Reading this vision was also a good reminder to challenge myself to take all the necessary steps to reverse engineer the outcomes I had chosen.

Every morning and every night I would visualize these outcomes as if they were already real. (You'll take an additional step I didn't figure out until later in Part 2, Training 13.) I wasn't doing it because I believed it would magically make it happen. I was doing it to get myself into the emotional and energetic state of bringing those outcomes to me. I knew that as long as I was stuck in this fight-or-flight stressed state, I would take action out of short-term scarcity instead of long-term abundance. The whole reason I had gotten myself into the mess I was in was because of short-term scarcity thinking, feeling, and decision-making.

Another tool I utilized was voice memos on my phone. I would talk things out with myself to have another cathartic release. Basically, I was my own therapist. I would speak all my frustrations, worries, and fears into my voice recorder as an emotional purge.

Finally, I leaned on a generally healthy lifestyle. I spent time with good friends, I walked and explored the city for hours at a time, I exercised in some form almost daily, and I ate nutritious Colombian foods. One thing I always understood was that my health was the foundation for everything both short- and long-term. Short-term was all about feeling good now, so I could perform my best. When I feel good, I focus better, I'm more creative, and I get more done. Additionally, I needed to keep my body on point if I wanted to find true love with one of these Colombian goddesses. Long-term I wanted to be around to experience the fruits of my labor. I was in the grind right now but knew that if I persisted I would eventually figure things out, and when that time came, I wanted to be healthy enough to enjoy it. After a couple of months in Colombia, I was beginning to get my footing.

THE POWER OF SURRENDER

After I had let go of trying to change the past, I had a renewed optimism and drive to move forward. I started to post some personal content on social media about the journey I had been on and started having conversations with people in my community sharing some of the powerful mental tools that had benefited me. This led me to pick up a few coaching clients and got me back to doing what I loved again. I was earning just enough money to make my debt payments and keep my head above water. At the time, I hadn't yet put together my complete training that you will get access to in Part 2, so a big part of what I was doing was helping people move through their core wound trauma.

Over the previous five years, I had invested in different coaches, workshops, and programs that had taught me some valuable tools in regard to releasing core wounds (we will explore this more later on), and they had done wonders for me. As a byproduct of healing my core wound, I went from feeling low-confidence and embarrassed to be in my own skin to feeling good about who I was and worthy of attracting a romantic mate. Keep in mind, though, I was a broke twenty-five-year-old, so I wasn't ready to settle down quite yet. Instead, I used my newfound confidence to date women and just have as much fun as possible in this new country while I figured out my career stuff.

The biggest gain I found from moving through my core wound was an acceptance of who I was and a surrendering of what I could not change. I was no longer ashamed of myself, and this was a game changer that I felt compelled to share with others. Since I took a non-traditional path to my education, everything I taught to my clients was first tested on me. If it worked for me I shared it with others. The more success I found with helping my coaching clients move through their core wounds, the more confident I felt in my ability to be this healer/coach guy full-time. I wasn't making a ton of money, but like I said, it was enough to make my debt payment and get by. I was surrendering my past failures and visualizing a more compelling future. I embraced the present moment and moved forward.

CHAPTER 10

THE POTENCY OF SINGULAR FOCUS

W HAT YOU FOCUS ON IS WHAT you get, and the more narrow your focus is, the more potent it becomes. Conversely, the more broad your focus becomes, the less potent it is. You can't focus on everything at once. Be strategic about what is worthy of your focus and when and where you should deploy it. If you focus on one thing, it will get 100 percent of your energy. That is what makes singular focus so powerful. If you are just starting down a path, it's important to give as much of your focus as possible to that one thing. After you have significant traction in one area, you can consider bringing in more things to focus on.

SELECTING A FOCUS

One afternoon I was introduced to a dude with a massive health and wellness social media following and online business who asked me if I would help him automate his Instagram account. I didn't know much about social media, but I was interested in learning more about building a social media audience. This experience was one of my wake-up calls as to how many people who were projecting a certain image into the world through social media are not who they say they are behind the brand. This guy was almost forty and was pushing a message of good ol' fashion Christian values aligned with healthy living. He was not a Christian and was down in Colombia partying his face off, doing cocaine, and having sex with eighteen-year-olds.

Nonetheless, I took on the gig in hopes of learning more about the space. I didn't love working with him, but what I learned from this experience was the power of building a social media following in a niche. Finding out what audience you want to serve is half the battle in building traction with an online brand. I also continued to learn the power of surrender as I felt myself in an undesirable position but knew it would only be for a short period of time. I took away the lessons that served me and discarded the rest. I was learning what made brands work online but also learned that I didn't want to be a dude who was saying one thing and doing another. After a few months of working together, we separated, and I was looking for my next opportunity to apply the lessons I had learned.

Shortly thereafter, one of my buddies who invited me down to Medellin was leading a month-long intensive in Barcelona, Spain, where he was teaching people how to build an online business. He invited me to come along for a free trip if I was willing to coach these people through the mindset roadblocks they would inevitably encounter as they took the leap into entrepreneurship. Free trip to Barcelona? Sold. I packed my bags and started the next adventure.

Upon arriving in Spain and being around people starting their businesses, I started to really understand the importance of singular focus and how consistency in a niche can lead to traction in a business. All the successful people around me had gotten traction by doing one thing and surrendering everything else. At the time my coaching business was doing okay, but it was not giving me the financial freedom I desired. I wanted to be able to pick and choose my clients based on what would be in both of our best interests instead of just taking on every client because I had bills to pay. The solution I came up with was to build an online social media brand using my passion for mental performance and physical wellness. The goal would be to go all in on this niche until

I had enough financial resources to get back to solely doing client work again from a place of financial freedom.

While brainstorming, I remembered how my buddy and I had captured lightning in a bottle, teaching our rooftop mindfulness workouts in Austin before I moved down to Colombia. My buddy and I had been in touch ever since I moved to Colombia and had been doing a podcast about mental and physical health together for fun the previous six months or so. One day on a call, I asked him if he would be willing to move down to Colombia and go all in to build a social media following and business around the concept of the rooftop workouts. He agreed, and a month later he had sold all his worldly belongings and met me back in Medellin to start the business. The idea was to expand upon this concept of exercise and mental performance together. He was already doing his side hustle teaching jump rope workouts, and that's what he would bring to the table. On my side, I would bring the mindset and meditation techniques to the brand. The first place we decided to start was through a YouTube channel we called Zen Dude Fitness. The niche would be jump rope and mindfulness. Mind/body workouts.

The crazy thing about taking the leap into being a public influencer on the internet was that I was still terrified of public speaking and had no skills or experience in this department. I was in such a state of desperation though that I didn't care. I just made videos that sucked and kept doing it and kept doing it until I started to get decent at it. This was again another example of how I was using consistent action to establish belief. The action I took started to build belief in my ability to be a public speaker and content creator. Through making over 1,000 videos on YouTube, I built the skill through pure conscious effort and will; as I mentioned in Chapter 5, this is not the most efficient way to reframe your belief system (the second way is coming up soon), but it does work.

After a few months, we had already hit a wall financially, and I had to make a decision. Previously, when I hit these walls in my businesses,

I just gave up. This time around things would be different. This was my burn-the-ships moment—there was no turning back. I committed to building a business with my buddy and had no plan B. I didn't care how long it took. I would do whatever was necessary to make this work.

Have you ever tried to commit to something but ended up backing out when things got tough and reverting back to what you believed to be an easier or safer course of action?

The power of metaphorically burning the ships is that you don't give your subconscious a way out. You are basically turning on the survival mechanism within yourself that will find success no matter what, because there is no alternative course of action available.

I knew that the path to success was through consistent singular focus. (More on how you can use this focus to systemize your goals is coming in Part 2, Training 15.) We both committed to one another and doubled down on the business together.

REFOCUSING

Lucky for us, this tech millionaire had found one of our Facebook fitness groups online and liked what we were doing. He sent us a random message and invited us to come out to Hawaii for the summer to train him and, in exchange, he would provide us with a place to stay and a car to use.

This was perfect timing for us, because our runway was pretty much gone. Honestly, I was out of money again, so this seemed like the only option. I encouraged my business partner to take the leap with me to train this guy in Hawaii to extend our runway. At first, he was skeptical, but after moving through those initial fears (of being sex slaves tortured in a basement), he agreed, and we used the last of our cash to book our flights to Hawaii. This turned out to be the perfect incubator for us, because there were zero distractions and the tech entrepreneur turned out to be an awesome dude with an incredibly kind family. We were staying in the sleepy town of Waimea on the Big Island of Hawaii, and there was literally nothing to do besides spend time in nature and build our YouTube channel.

After a slow start and banging our heads against our desk to figure out how to get traction on YouTube, we finally came across a piece of knowledge that changed the game for us. One of my buddies at the time had recently launched an SEO company and offered to give me his course for free. As I started going through it, I had an *AHA!* moment like none before.

Google and YouTube were there to answer people's questions...
But no one was answering the questions about jump rope fitness.

Although jump rope fitness was not the exact path I wanted to take, I saw this as the only option for getting traction at the time, and we doubled down into the niche of jump rope fitness. We started to type into the YouTube search bar "How to jump rope" and the terms would auto-generate. "How to jump rope for boxing." "How to jump rope to lose weight." "How to jump rope for beginners." YouTube was telling us the exact content to make, whereas previously we were just making videos that we thought were helpful. Almost immediately after starting to make those auto-generated videos, we started seeing traction for the first time.

Within three months, we had gone from less than a thousand subscribers to over five thousand subscribers, and there was light at the end of the tunnel. The only problem for me was that we were drifting farther and farther away from my passion and going deeper into the jump rope fitness niche. At this point, I came back to my decision to go all in with a singular focus. I decided to stay focused on doing something that would provide me with financial stability while helping other people achieve their fitness goals, with the vision of coming back to my true calling when the time was right.

GAINING TRACTION

A girl from Colombia, who I had started dating before I'd left, came to visit me in Hawaii. One morning at the coffee shop, she decided that she wanted to add a bagel with cream cheese to her normal order of hot chocolate. I felt a sharp pain of anxiety in my solar plexus. I knew that I only had $7.00 in my bank account and getting a bagel with cream cheese meant that it would cost me around $7.50. This led to a very awkward moment where I eventually had to confess to her that I was flat broke. I felt completely emasculated when I told her I didn't have another dollar to spend that day, but I was optimistic and told her that if she stuck with me, I knew that my business would break through soon. Although confused, she liked me enough to accept that she was dating a broke gringo, and at the end of it, the only damage done was to my ego (we'll get into ego death in Chapter 13). We went back to Colombia, and I moved into her mom's 500-square-foot apartment. I was a twenty-six-year-old with no money in my bank account, but hope in my heart.

Fortunately for me, one place where my subconscious was aligned was in romantic relationships. My parents had modeled a healthy relationship for me, and this actually came easy to me. Although I had a bunch of my own emotional issues to still work through, I at least could hold the space in a relationship that kept our bond strong. By this time, I had already overstayed my Colombian visa, and so I very nonchalantly asked my girlfriend if she wanted to marry me, so I could stay in the country. Technically we got a free union, which is a step down from real marriage. Definitely not the most romantic proposal any woman hopes for, but she agreed, and although we weren't married in our minds, we took another step in our relationship so I could get my visa and stick around to see where this relationship and this business might go.

By the time the new year rolled around, the YouTube channel was panning out better than we could have ever imagined. We had 50,000 subscribers and officially had the necessary traction to sustain our business. We were making over $10,000 a month and, best of all, had a community of raving fans supporting us from all over the world. I still was barely getting by, because my business partner had given the business a loan from his savings, so most of the money we were receiving now went to paying him back. I was, however, making enough money to finally move out of my mother-in-law's house and get my own place with my wife. We moved into a high-rise apartment and started a new chapter together where I could breathe a little easier and live with a little less anxiety.

CHAPTER 11
BREAKING GENERATIONAL CURSES

THE BODY TALKS, AND IF WE don't listen to it, there will be consequences. When you do the underlying work in Part 2, to see your self-limiting programming for what it is, you will gain the intuitive connection to do what's best for your body when it speaks to you. It all starts with how you feel. When you feel at peace in the present, you know you are in alignment and doing what is best for your body.

When you don't feel good, either physically or emotionally, you risk turning on genes for illnesses that you may be predisposed to. The field of study that explores this is called Epigenetics. Epigenetics explains how all of us have a predisposed genetic code that may encompass various illnesses, but the illnesses lay dormant until the body goes under enough stress (physical or emotional) to turn those pieces of code on. To take it one step further, I would add that the code we carry with us is not just wrapped up in our DNA. It's also our inherited subconscious programming, which is commonly referred to as generational trauma and curses. The only way to break those curses is by facing the self-limiting programming we inherited and transmuting it into self-empowering programming. If you haven't picked up on it yet, that's exactly what we are doing here with this book and the journey you are currently on with me. Poor genetics is just another way we have been programmed to fail, but the good news is that epigenetics tells us that there is something we can do about it.

THE PROGRAMMING IN OUR DNA

Coming up on twenty-seven years old, I was still living in the shame of not having much to show for my five years of entrepreneurship. I couldn't help but play the comparison game a little bit, watching my friends from college get good-paying jobs, buy homes, and live with a level of financial security. Although I was getting traction in my business, I couldn't quite afford to live outside of Colombia yet, and this compelled me to work my face off, so I could graduate to my next stage of life. When we rebranded our company to the Jump Rope Dudes, to capitalize on our growing fitness niche, the work I do now in the mental performance space was completely removed from the company. It was then that I was introduced to how powerful the mind can be as it relates to deteriorating your health when you ignore your body's needs.

On paper, things were going better for me than ever before. My relationship with my now wife was amazing and my business was thriving, but somehow I felt worse than ever before. I was feeling so lethargic and depressed. Rationally, I was trying to put the pieces together to explain this, but nothing seemed to make sense. I was trapped in this dark place and couldn't see any way out. Despite feeling terrible, I kept pushing. I kept working. I didn't give up on my initial intention of staying focused on this business until I got to a place of financial freedom. Soon we were making enough money to finally move back to the USA. We moved to Los Angeles, believing that this was the place to be if we wanted to be successful YouTubers.

I was still dealing with these feelings of lethargy and depression but pushed forward believing it was something I just needed to endure. It wasn't until I saw a doctor and had blood work done that everything made perfect sense. I had a hypoactive thyroid, which was leading to all my symptoms. This made sense, given that my mom and brother had the same issue, and within a couple of weeks of being on medication I was fully healed and finally feeling like myself again.

Reflecting back on this experience, it was now obvious that the previous five years of excessive intermittent fasting, too much coffee, too much stress, and too much work had pushed my body to a point where those genes for my thyroid disorder were finally turned on. Here is where I started to uncover the connection between our emotional states and how they can affect our existing genetic code.

My mom had grown up in an abusive household where she was not allowed to speak her truth. The thyroid is located where the throat chakra is and correlates with your ability to speak your truth. When the throat chakra is clogged up, you can't speak your truth, and you suppress your real feelings, and if you apply enough pressure, as I did, you can create a physical abnormality from this, which was my thyroid disorder.

The body is tied in with the subconscious and will carry subconscious repression with it through generations. When I asked my Mom about her ability to speak her truth, she shared with me that when she was a young girl and woman, she was so terrified of speaking in class that she would freeze up and get beet red in the face—the same way I did. What this told me was that many of my subconscious programs were put in me even before I was born. These programs were running within my mom, and since she never did the reprogramming work to release herself from them, they got passed right along to me.

Through many conversations with my father about self-worth, insecurities, and fear around money, I can see how so much of my programming had been picked up from him as well. I had a tremendous amount of resistance and blocks around being able to make money, and that was obviously inherited from his fears and experiences.

Some of the issues we can manifest are a byproduct of not just our experience but the experience of our ancestors. Just like we get passed along traits like blue eyes and big noses, we also pass along unresolved emotional trauma that can manifest itself in emotional and physical abnormalities. Deep down, we are talking about the same issue of self-limiting subconscious programming. Only this programming is inherited before we are even born. An example personal to me is my Jewish ancestors on my father's side. It is well documented that the Jews have been persecuted throughout history and that fear of being harmed for who we are runs deep in our DNA. Being anxious was my default way of being, and it is still the default way of being for all my Jewish relatives. None of us chose this. It's just who we were programmed to be. Until one relative does the work to transcend these anxious tendencies, they will continue to be passed down from one generation to the next despite the fact that none of us who are now alive have actually lived through the same persecution of our ancestors. Depending on your own lineage, you can probably track down the trauma that has been passed down to you through your DNA.

So the good and bad news is that you don't choose most of your programming. Some programming comes through your genetics, some comes through early childhood experiences, and some comes through your own lived experience as an adult. The bad news is that you can't control what self-sabotaging programming gets passed along to you. The good news is that if you have the courage, you can change it. The other good news is that the fact that you are alive today says a lot about how incredible your programming actually is. Think about it, thousands of generations had to survive for you to get here today, which tells you that despite some minor flaws, your programming is quite miraculous. Let's sit into the gratitude of what our ancestors have had to overcome and honor them by carrying the torch forward.

What I didn't realize at the time is that part of my thyroid disorder was stemming from the fact that I stopped speaking my truth—with my mental performance content stripped out of Jump Rope Dudes, I had no real voice in my work. In a way, I had repeated the same pattern from my previous business. The only difference was that this time I was actually making enough money to pay my bills.

The lack of speaking my truth and the physical stress I had put on my body had triggered my subconscious to turn on the gene for hypothyroidism, but lucky for me this disorder can be resolved by taking a small pill every morning. My hope is that you are able to learn from my experience, though, and that you will listen to what your body needs when it speaks to you. The human body is an incredible organism that always asks for what it needs. We just have to slow down and listen.

Reflecting inwardly, can you think about something you are suppressing or ignoring in your life right now that could lead to mental or physical issues down the line? Now would be a good time to address what has been suppressed and start to take the necessary steps to get yourself into alignment with how you know you need to be showing up in your life.

CHAPTER 12
CONSISTENCY IS KING

I T MAY SOUND OVERLY SIMPLISTIC, BUT the main reason most people fail is that they give up. If you can cultivate the mental skills to persevere through the hard times and keep going, you will position yourself to eventually step into the life you are seeking. The key, though, is to stay focused on a specific direction or goal. If you start and stop all the time, you will be throwing away all the momentum you have built up. Envision the path ahead and do all the necessary inner work to sustain yourself until your goals become your new reality.

YOU CAN'T FAIL IF YOU DON'T GIVE UP

Shortly after figuring out my health issues, my financial troubles were coming to an end as well. The clear outcome I had set around money had come to fruition and, in doing so, had built the belief in my ability to make money as an entrepreneur. I was finally able to pay off all my debt, and I was free. After making that final payment, I went and leased a brand new jeep, which felt like a physical trophy to represent the inner journey I had been on. After arriving home, I sat in my car and cried my eyes out in a deep cathartic release.

The past three years, I had been carrying the weight of that debt and the failure attached to it, and when I made that final payment, it felt like the weight of the world was taken off of my shoulders. I was free—free from needing to do anything out of survival. From this place of financial freedom, I felt compelled to start stepping back into the coaching space once again to align myself with my unique talents.

I would keep running Jump Rope Dudes, because it was paying my bills, but I would now divert some of my energy back to what I loved most. The previous year, I had been inspired by the movie *Creed* to get into boxing. By the time I got to Los Angeles, I had some beginner skills and had started training at one of the top boxing gyms that housed professional boxers. Through my time there, I fell in love with boxing and started to build coaching relationships with some of the pros training at my gym. Historically, boxers are poor until they get to the very tippy top of their sport, and then the money comes. There are maybe fifty boxers in the world who can actually make a comfortable living just from their sport alone. For this reason, I started to offer my services to these pros for free. These guys were the perfect case studies for me because they compete in one of the most mentally demanding sports in the world and usually have a lot of self-inhibiting programming that needs to be re-engineered to get to their goals. Even though I wasn't yet reaching my goal of making money with mental coaching, I was finally getting into the big leagues. My dream of working with pro athletes that started eight years earlier was now becoming my reality, thanks to this clear GPS destination I had set within my subconscious and a relentless will to succeed.

I started down the path with one boxer in particular who had all the physical potential in the world but kept sabotaging himself in the moments that counted the most. The first part of our work together was moving him through his core wound in the same way that I had moved through my own. (I want to note here that as my evolution progressed, I learned that the core wound itself does not even need to be addressed in the reprogramming process. It's the corresponding self-defeating programming that stems from the core wound that holds you back. As long as you deal with the programming, you are free and that core wound holds no power over you. We'll explore how to do that in Part 2, Training 10.) The result was life-changing. When he released this massive blockage, everything started to flow for him almost immediately, and he was offered an opportunity to be a part of a tournament-style reality TV show where he would be able to potentially compete for a championship belt if he won the tournament. He carried the momentum of our work together into the show and began dominating his opponents. Unfortunately, they cut him off from all outside communication while they filmed, and that is where our work stopped.

He made it all the way to the championship fight that was at the Los Angeles Lakers basketball arena, and in that fight, I saw that there was still work to be done. In the biggest moment of his career, he showed up as a shadow of himself and basically gave away the fight and lost by decision. It was by no means a rational choice for him to not put on his best performance. Unfortunately, his subconscious was running the show, and that led to him getting overly stressed out before the fight and flooding his body with way too much adrenaline. The byproduct was a flat performance where his explosive reflexes were not accessible to him like they usually were. He was not able yet to be consistent in his performance. Despite feeling regret about not being able to guide him through this experience and coach him in the championship, I realized that the work that he had yet to do was the same work that I still needed to do on myself. He was a mirror for the growth I still needed to facilitate in my own inner world. I had not yet cleaned up my own inner world, and so I did not yet have the capacity to help someone else do the same. (You'll learn how to systemize this for success in Part 2, Training 15—a key takeaway to be consistent with your actions.)

To get myself to a place where I understood this process, I went seeking my next breakthrough, and holy shit, did it come.

CHAPTER 13
THE EGO IS NOT YOUR ENEMY

T HE EGO—OUR SENSE OF SELF—IS NOT our enemy. The ego is just a filtration system for life that we use to make internal representations. It is our subconscious programming that determines what representations we make when we see, hear, smell, taste, and touch the world around us. Without the ego, we are at one with everything, which is a beautiful experience, but it is not the human experience. We are here to be human and interact with the world through this egoic interface.

There is no way to viscerally understand the ego until you have an ego death—aka transcending your understanding of self—but trust me when I say that it's not a part of you that needs to be removed. It's a part of you that needs to be utilized correctly by reprogramming the underlying programming that makes the ego act out of integrity with who you want to be. Finally, an ego death is something that I believe all adults should go through at some point in their lives. It humbles you and makes you appreciate the sacredness of the human experience. Furthermore, it connects you to a power greater than yourself that allows you to let go of some of the pressure you are putting on yourself, because you know you are not alone. If you feel drawn to experiencing an ego death, I discuss it more in Part 2, Training 2.

DISCOVERING WHO YOU TRULY ARE
Around the time that I was seeking my next spiritual awakening, Mike Tyson was launching his podcast *Hot Boxin' with Mike Tyson*.

I immediately gravitated toward his show because of his ability to be fully authentic without the fear of judgment from others. This is something I was working on at the time and enjoyed learning from his ability to let it all hang out. Interestingly enough, Mike decided to bring on a shaman in the first episode of his podcast, where he was guided through a ceremony with the venom from the Bufo Alvarius Toad (chemical compound 5MeO-DMT.)

One of my favorite lines from this podcast was Mike recanting his thoughts upon smoking the Toad during the ceremony: "Oh no! I took this shit, and this white boy killed me!" His recollection of the experience is hilarious, but there was a deeper truth he was sharing in those words. He felt like he had been killed because his ego had died in that experience. The truth is we do need our ego. Without it, we would be floating in the abyss of infinite energy without the ability to perceive the world around us. The ego is the mechanism that allows us to hold the conscious experience of being a human. But one of the main side effects of smoking the Bufo Toad is that you lose all sense of self and identity. Who you believe you are vanishes at a moment's notice, and you are launched into a space of pure being and nothingness. This is what it means to have an ego death. The you that you have associated yourself with your entire life disappears, and it reveals an essence of you that goes beyond your ego. I would call this essence your spirit, but you can call it whatever you want. As you get into the training, I will share how having an ego-death experience can be a major catalyst for your growth, because it allows you to observe your subconscious programming without judgment. Needless to say, it can be quite a life-altering experience.

For whatever reason, I knew that it was my destiny to smoke this Toad as well. As I have previously stated, I don't believe in coincidences. I believe everything happens as a byproduct of natural law, and the fact that I was seeking an awakening aligned perfectly with hearing about Mike's experience. Little did I know that the experience I'm about to share was the catalyst for how I learned how to do all the reprogramming work I will be walking you through in Part 2. A week or two later, I was at a hippie event in Venice Beach where we were doing conscious connection exercises like deep eye gazing. I immediately had the intuition that this would be the perfect place to start asking around about getting access to an experience with the Toad. After we finished the exercises, a few of us sat down at a picnic table to eat our lunch together. I floated it out there. "Has anyone ever smoked the Toad?" In perfect synchronicity, the kid across from me knew a shaman who was hosting ceremonies a few hours outside of Los Angeles. Perfect. I took the contact information and reached out immediately.

EXPLORATION

Within a week, I arrived at this shaman lady's house with around seven other people I had never met before. I had minimal expectations about what I was about to go through. I knew that no one dies smoking the Toad, and that was enough for me. We sat in a circle, and my heart started beating like crazy. The ceremony started, and the first person volunteered to receive the medicine. I watched as the shaman heated up this Toad venom in a pipe and then gave it to the first person to inhale. He inhaled, sat back, and—poof—was gone. His eyes were closed, and his body was there, but it was obvious that his conscious awareness was no longer in his body. The shaman proceeded to do some chanting and waving of indigenous feathers as this dude lay motionless on the floor, having his experience. The shaman assistant proceeded to blast the didgeridoo into this guy's ears from behind, and we all held the space for his experience. Holding space is a spiritual way of saying we sat around attentively in the present moment giving this person our love, care, and attention. Fifteen minutes later, he came back to conscious awareness with a smile of ecstasy on his face and a glow of infinite love. So far, so good. This calmed my nerves a bit.

After a few more people had similar experiences, the torch was passed my way, and it was time for me to meet the Toad. Before smoking it, my heart started beating faster and faster. I knew this was going to break my perception of reality in a way that I had never experienced before. My rational mind would be completely overridden, and that's exactly what I wanted. I wanted to experience letting go of all control. The reason I was called to the Toad in the first place was that when you smoke the Toad, you don't have a choice in whether you resist the medicine or not. This is one of the most powerful psychedelics known to man, and in the short fifteen-minute experience, you get ripped right out of your ego and get taken right to the source of all life. I was ready for it—or as ready as I'd ever be.

I pressed the pipe to my lips, inhaled, leaned back, and I was gone.

The man that I had spent my whole life identifying with and protecting vanished in a matter of seconds. I was now in this space of infinite awareness and connection beyond anything that could be explained in rational thought or language. I just was. I was with it. It was with me. For the first time in my life, I was experiencing a true ego death. Everything I had known about the world I had spent twenty-eight years living in was immediately put into question. I was in this space of pure being. It felt like a split second, but apparently, it was fifteen minutes. As I started to come back into some form of conscious awareness, I heard the didgeridoo behind me blasting energy through my body. My body immediately started convulsing. My body was releasing energy that had been stored within me and my ancestors for generations. My conscious mind tried to grasp back control, and the more it did, the more my body would convulse. This medicine was giving me exactly what I had asked for. It was taking my control away completely and forcing me to just be.

A few minutes later, I started to sit up in disbelief at what had just happened to me. Nothing I experienced could be put into words, but I knew I had unfinished business. I met eyes with the shaman, and she already knew what I was going to say. I needed to immediately go back in for a second dose. My previously programmed identity was still ing for the illusion of what was, and I wanted to fully transcend into a new way of being.

As my Irish buddy likes to say, "If you're gonna do it, do it right!"

I pressed the pipe to my lips again, inhaled, held it, and then sat back into nothingness as once again my ego disappeared, and I was in union with what I would now call the oneness (more on this in Chapter 15). An undeniable sense of connection to something bigger than myself. Something beyond the Me that I had grown accustomed to attaching myself to. I was still there with a unique awareness of energy, but I no longer had my five senses to experience what was happening. I just was. It just was. I was at one with the whole big show. Again, as I came back to conscious awareness, I began to have visions of sitting around a fire with my ancestors, and I felt like they were there holding the space for me to undergo this transformation.

The sound of the didgeridoo in my ear lit me the fuck up again, and my body began convulsing uncontrollably once again. My ego tried to regain control, and I began to think to myself that I must be pretty special to have to go through so much suffering when I had just watched these people have such peaceful experiences. The ego tends to do this. Whenever it loses control, it wants to make itself feel special to justify our need to identify with it. In this moment, though, I didn't want the ego experience. I wanted to simply be with the infinite energy source and allow that experience to anchor into me. The Toad pulled me out of my myopic view of the world so I could see that life wasn't happening to me; I was creating my life.

THE EGO IS YOUR FRIEND WHEN YOU ARE ALIGNED

You may have heard before that the ego is the enemy.

This was my first experience of actually understanding the ego's purpose, and although it was fighting for control, I could feel that the ego was not my enemy, rather it was a survival mechanism necessary to navigate the human experience. I was grateful for my ego and had so

99

much more understanding for what its purpose truly is.

After a few minutes, my portion of the ceremony was over, and I had just undergone the most powerful, and to be fair, traumatizing experience of my entire life. One of the shaman assistants sat me outside in the sun and gave me an apple to connect me back to something organic and earthly. I thought this was kind of funny because what had just become apparent to me was that it was all organic. Everyone was connected, and there was nothing more earthly about an apple than there was about my iPhone. It all came from the same source. Everything is a byproduct of this all-encompassing energy field—the grass I was sitting on and the aluminum siding of the house. It all seemed the same to me. Everything was sacred in its own way.

In thirty minutes, I went from not having much of a spiritual belief to knowing with certainty that God was real. Not the dogmatic God we often hear about, but God as the all-encompassing infinite energetic intelligence that is producing and running through everything that ever is, was, or will be. This God cannot truly be spoken of. Only experienced.

Once I got my feet under me, I realized I couldn't put into words what I had just experienced and felt extremely unsettled. I wanted answers. I wanted advice. I wanted to know what to do with my life moving forward after undergoing such a challenging experience. I didn't get what I wanted. We were sent on our way without much closure, and I spent the next three hours driving home wondering what the fuck just happened and what I could do to integrate the experience I just had.

I was raw, vulnerable, and fully cracked open. This openness created space for my previously hidden subconscious programming to flood into my conscious awareness. I was EVERYTHING and I was NOTHING. *What did it mean? What do I do now? Where do I go from here?* Upon returning home, I started trying to put the pieces back together again.

CHAPTER 14
UNCOVERING YOUR HIDDEN PROGRAMMING

Y OUR SUBCONSCIOUS PROGRAMMING IS THE DRIVER of your behavior and, as a result, the outcomes of your life. Negative thinking and behavior patterns will only change when the underlying programming changes. This doesn't require you to be someone you are not. It just requires that you go into your subconscious to identify where there is resistance toward the outcomes you want in your life. Once you find that resistance, you will find the beliefs, which act as pieces of code in your supercomputer subconscious mind.

Once those beliefs are transmuted to work for you instead of against you, there is a feeling of intrinsic motivation and clarity to get yourself where you want to be. It doesn't require force. It feels like flow. It feels natural. It feels like coming home to who you truly are. At its core, we are talking about going into your shadow and doing mental alchemy. Most people run away from their shadow, but that is where all the gold is! We must reprogram ourselves to see our inner darkness or shadow as a part of ourselves that just needs to be reclaimed. By going into your self-limiting programming and transmuting it to become self-empowering programming, you take over the steering wheel for your life.

CLEANING UP YOUR INNER PLANET
When I got home, I immediately tried my best to articulate the experience I had to my wife, but any explanation in words just sounded like

gobbly goop. I was grasping for control of the uncontrollable. Trying to explain the unexplainable. That night I went to bed with my mind racing and quickly learned that the Bufo Toad wasn't quite done with me yet.

Starting that night and for the following couple weeks, I would have these types of experiences every night where I would wake up in a cold sweat, screaming and scaring my wife half to death. It felt like when I was asleep, I would actually leave my body and go into another dimension, so coming out of those experiences was extremely startling to me. Hence the scream and cold sweats. They were unlike any dreams I had ever experienced before.

After doing some googling, I found out that these intense dreams were a very common occurrence. It's called the echo of the ceremony. To be honest, I dreaded going to sleep every night because these experiences were so intense and oftentimes frightening. One night I felt like I was levitating above my bed, and in a fit of panic, I woke up and jumped out of bed.

My anxiety was super high from all the bubbling up from my subconscious, and sometimes it would get so intense that I felt panicked. It was time to bring out the big guns. I called my Sensei up and told him we had work to do. He agreed to start training me again to move through this experience, and our work began.

In the first session, he asked me how intense the feelings were that I still had in regard to this Bufo experience, and I told him 10/10 intense. He smiled and looked at me with a soft gaze, and a few seconds later, I began laughing uncontrollably. He asked me how intense the feelings were now, and I said 0/10! Believe what you want, but he had just gone into my subconscious and pulled out the trauma that I had been carrying since the ceremony. This may sound crazy if you have never experienced anything like this before, but this is simply what mastery over the skill of mental alchemy looks like. In my coaching, I can do this with my clients, but it requires a lot more of their active participation.

Since my Sensei had been practicing these techniques for over twenty years, he could do it for me without my participation.

From there, the real work began as he introduced to me this concept of the inner planet. He explained that we all live on our own subconscious inner planets that, just like nature, are perfect by default. Yes, there may be chaos in nature, but it's all purposeful, and it operates under natural laws that work in harmony. When we disrupt nature on our own inner planet by interjecting self-limiting subconscious programming, it's the equivalent of pouring sewage and toxic waste all over our inner planet. We need to clean up this self-limiting programming to reveal the true and natural state of our nature. What we were doing with work together was identifying the beliefs that were working against me and transmuting them into new beliefs that would work for me. For example, I could believe that the economy is holding me back from making money, or I could believe, regardless of what is happening in the economy, I can still make money. The first belief is trash because it makes you a victim of circumstances, whereas the second belief is like a naturally occurring piece of nature because it allows me to deal with reality as it is without attaching a self-limiting story to it. As you can imagine, this is a deep rabbit hole you can go down and, fortunately, my fitness business and my accompanying finances were in a space of stability where I could step back from my work and go all in on cleaning up my inner planet.

Over the next couple of weeks, we spent hours every day diving deep into my subconscious to reveal all my self-limiting beliefs (programming). (You will be doing this soon, in Part 2, Training 10). Oftentimes, in the spiritual community, people refer to this type of work as facing your shadow. The only way we can face this shadow is by going all the way into it and seeing it for what it truly is. My Sensei started the process with me by prompting me to complete phrases like "I believe I am." At first, I had so much resistance to what lay beneath the surface that nothing came up. He explained to me that this wasn't a fast food exercise. It wasn't something I could use my thinking mind to do. We were sitting down to a twelve-course meal, and it was going to take time to uncover what had been hidden beneath the surface for all my life. After over ten years of meditating, learning healing modalities, and helping others on their journey, this was quite the ego death in itself to uncover how much work I still had to do on myself.

We continued with the prompting exercise.

"I believe I am—WORTHLESS" Oof. That was like a knife to the gut.

Where did that come from?
I continued.

"I believe I am:
A loser.
Good for nothing.
Stupid.
Lost.
Confused.
Helpless."

Holy shit! I thought.

My whole life, I had been operating from a place of fear. No wonder I had sabotaged myself so much. No wonder I had no confidence growing up. No wonder I didn't want to be seen. No wonder I didn't believe I could be successful. We then moved into my beliefs around money.

I believe money is: bad, useful, necessary, power, greed, self-worth, freedom, the ability to focus, and a long-term game.

Jeesh! No wonder I struggled to hit my breakthrough money goals. I believed money was bad, it would make me greedy, and it was needed to define my self-worth. We then moved into relationships. I believe relationships are scary, risky, hopeless, not worth the time, and stupid.

Man oh man, I thought. *I am so fucked that it's* almost *funny.*

This process in itself was almost a greater ego death than smoking the Toad. I wanted to believe that I was so evolved because of my diligent self-development over the years and, to my credit, I had come a very long way. Through the tools I had shared up until this point, I was able to build a healthy body, a healthy romantic relationship, and a healthy bank account. This was just another level I had to move through to unlock the rest of my vision and the inner peace I always knew was possible.

As I mentioned earlier, there are two ways to rewrite your belief system at the subconscious level. The first way is by just forcing yourself to do the things you don't believe you can do until you force success and that repeated success creates new beliefs. Forcing things through a conscious will is not a bad thing. It's how I was able to create positive outcomes in my life before I learned the second path to create belief in myself. However, the first path is the path of most resistance, and many of us can get lost in the chaos of it all. The second way is by simply going into your subconscious and rewriting the software that runs your life, which is the path I was now embarking on. By taking the second path, clarity emerges, and the pain we experience can be internalized as a teacher instead of something that feels like a never-ending cycle of suffering.

YOUR BELIEFS ARE YOUR PROGRAMMING

The dark side of not intentionally choosing your beliefs is that you become a victim of circumstances. As you have learned from my story, most of the programming we get is not in alignment with living in a state of peace and abundance. The reason is that a lot of belief systems have been implemented into societies through fear. When we look back at the colonization of countries all over the world, we see that incredibly rich cultures were forced to give up the wisdom of their ancestors to survive in the new world of their colonizers. From the indigenous in North America to South America to Africa to India to pretty much every corner of the planet, you can find rich cultures that were forced to assimilate their belief systems to avoid being murdered. Just because you grew up with a belief system that was passed down to you by people who care for you does not mean it's in your best interest to follow in their footsteps. As you audit your inner world, find the resistance within yourself and challenge the beliefs that are no longer serving the highest expression of who you can be.

If I wanted to make a quantum leap in my life, I knew I had to change these beliefs that had bubbled up to the surface. This right here is where most personal development, psychedelic experiences, and therapy fall short. They get you to a certain level of awareness, but they don't actually help you clearly identify the underlying programming that is sabotaging you so you can transmute it. I will give you the keys to do so in Part 2.

Let me clarify now the relationship between beliefs and subconscious programming. Our beliefs are like pieces of code that write the subconscious programming that runs our lives. In a way, they act as a filtration mechanism for your experienced reality. Whatever you believe to be true is true for you, because you will make it so.

Can you think about a belief that you hold that has caused unnecessary suffering in your life?

What about an uncommon belief that has served you?

In my own life, one belief that caused me unnecessary suffering was the belief that the unknown is going to cause me pain in the future. Holding this belief led to a lot of stagnation and a lack of action toward my goals because I was afraid of what the unknown would do to me.

I transmuted that limiting belief into the unknown is going to bring me growth and pleasure. Now I run toward the unknown because I know it's going to lead to my personal evolution and the highest expression of who I can be.

An uncommon belief that has always served me is that everything is happening for my best interest. Because I've always believed this to be true, I have always been the eternal optimist.

Beliefs very much create your reality, and so that is why when we are looking to change our self-limiting subconscious programming, we focus on changing our beliefs.[8]

During the next three months, I went all in on changing every bit of programming that was not serving me. The first step, of course, was acceptance. Accepting what was, so it could be changed. That is a whole process in itself (as you will see in Part 2, Training 11). After that was surrendering the old identity that was being held within my limiting beliefs. Surrender is just another word for letting go—releasing what no longer serves us.

Next, it was the transmutation process of going into my subconscious and choosing new beliefs to replace the old ones I had just released (see Part 2, Training 12). This process is mechanical in theory, but there is a lot of art built into the process. What you do is choose a belief (piece of programming) that is the polar opposite of the belief you are trying to transcend. This works with the law of polarity.

This is easy when it comes to a belief like "I am worthless."

The opposite is "I am more than enough" or "I am worthy."

The art in the process is choosing the right beliefs when things come up that have nuance. For example, I noticed that every time my wife would be in pain from a stomachache, headache, or whatever, I would feel bad. The reason was that I believed I was responsible for—and in control of—the way she felt. I changed my belief to only being responsible for the way I felt. Coming back to the core of my training, this couldn't be more true. We are all only in control of our own focus and choices. When we try to control other people, we are playing a losing game. Even if you have the best intentions in the world and do everything in your power to help someone, you really can't control how they feel.

---

8   A doctor who has done extensive research on this is Dr. Bruce Lipton. To learn more about the mechanics of this, I highly recommend his book *The Biology of Belief*. https://www.brucelipton.com/books/biology-of-belief/

If this sounds like quite the process, it is. I have over thirty pages, and counting, of beliefs I have had to transmute to work for me instead of against me. The higher and further I strive on my journey, the more resistance I encounter in the form of self-limiting beliefs. There will always be these self-imposed ceilings that we will need to break through to unlock higher emotional states of being and achievement. Think of it this way: The prerequisite to graduating onto the next level of life is moving through that self-limiting programming. Whenever you are striving for more, you can expect to encounter it. When it shows up, it shouldn't be a surprise. It's just like playing a video game. You're going to have to overcome the boss at the end of every level to unlock the next level. The reason that you continue to run into self-limiting beliefs as you strive for more is that your subconscious wants you to stay in a state of homeostasis. Your subconscious recognizes that what you believe now has kept you alive, and so it doesn't want to change anything that could threaten your survival. If you ask the average person how they are doing, they will think about it and do mental math in their head adding up what's going well and what's not going well to give you their answer. They might think to themselves, *Well, my family is generally healthy, and I am making a decent living, so I'm good.* Unfortunately, that doesn't get to the core of why you are actually feeling good or bad. You can't think your way into feeling better. You must feel your way there. You must be able to feel the anxiety in your body and go into the feeling far enough to get to a place where you can ask yourself, "What am I believing to be true that would make me feel this way?" From there, you have to be able to sit into the tension until the answer reveals itself. No thinking required.

We live in a fast food culture where we want everything right now, which is what makes this so challenging for many of us, but if we have the courage to sit into our resistance, our bodies will always show us where we need to make a shift. (We will explore this more in Part 2, Training 1.)

After three months of dedicating myself to this work, there was still this itching anxiety inside of me that wanted more clarity about what the bigger purpose was to this all.

This led me to the defining experience of my life that left me with absolute clarity and the ability to finally be the alchemist of my own programming.

CHAPTER 15
BECOMING THE ALCHEMIST

I T'S BAKED INTO US TO BELIEVE in a higher power, and many of us already do, but for those of us who don't, here is a rational framework that will make it tangible and useful for you. When you believe there is something beyond yourself handling the bigger existential game, you can put your energy into only the things that you can truly control: your focus and your choices. I call this governing energy the oneness. You can call it whatever you want. Just as long as you trust it enough to give up needing to control the uncontrollable. There is no one judging your actions. There is just your intuitive experience of life and your ability to trust the purity of your heart to guide you where you are meant to be.

Once you understand that you are connected to the oneness, you will also understand that your own self-limiting programming is the only thing holding you back—then it is time to transmute that energy. The key to subconscious reprogramming is to flip the polarity of the energy that has been holding you back from what you desire most. Once that programming (in the form of beliefs) is flipped, you step into alignment with the energetic frequency necessary for you to clearly see the actions required to get to your desired outcomes. Energy cannot be created or destroyed, which is why we must reclaim the energy that was previously holding us back. The energy will never just disappear. It needs to be redirected. This is what the sages call mental alchemy. This is exactly how you become the master of your own life.

THE UNIVERSAL TRUTH THAT WE ARE ALL CONNECTED

This itching existential angst was something that I had carried with me for all my life. It always felt like there was something missing or some greater truth that I had yet to discover. Although the experience with the Bufo Toad opened my mind to a higher power and gave me something to surrender to, I still felt this curiosity to better viscerally understand what that something greater was.

To explore this, I decided to take a heroic dose of mushrooms by myself to pass back through this veil separating me from this greater intelligence in hopes of getting the clarity that I had been yearning for.

Forty-five minutes after taking the mushrooms, I felt my consciousness shifting, and I closed my eyes to go deeper into the experience. I began to feel very similar to how I felt when I smoked the Bufo Toad, but with more control this time around.

As I went deeper into my experience, I passed into another space that disconnected me from my ego and allowed me to become fully immersed in the experience at hand. For those unfamiliar with these altered states of consciousness this may sound strange, but it was like an entity of some sort was guiding me to the truth that I was seeking. It immersed me in this circulating energy representing the cyclical nature of everything and everyone in the universe. It was like this entity was treating me like a child who wanted to see what his parents were doing behind closed doors. The entity obliged and kept showing me this representation of the oneness, and I found myself saying the mantra "the oneness, the oneness, the oneness." I repeated this mantra over and over and over and over as I felt it being programmed deep into my cells until all of the sudden I was jolted awake by a powerful energetic wave that hit me from behind.

I looked behind me and blinked repeatedly, trying to regain focus on what or who was behind me.

As my vision became clearer, I saw that a framed photo on my wall had just fallen off its hook onto another framed photo on my wall that was hanging beneath it. The photo that fell said, "You are exactly where you need to be," and the photo it was now resting on was the enso symbol that represents The Oneness.

If this wasn't a sign, I don't know what is.

I can't explain or rationalize what happened in that room in the moment in which that happened, but what I can tell you is that the message was received. The higher power I had been seeking that represented the bigger game I was playing was smack dab right in front of my face.

The Oneness.

The understanding that everything and everyone is all connected in this greater overarching intelligent infinite governing energy field. Call it God. Call it Source. Call it the ALL. Call it whatever you want, but this is what I could surrender my human experience to. A power greater than myself that connected me to this greater energy. I felt it in my bones that my ego experience of being a human was not the beginning and not the end. It was simply a drop of water in the greater ocean of the ALL. Everything just made sense, and for the first time in my life, I was no longer seeking the truth. I had found my way home. I was now living in the truth.

There was no religion or ideology necessary to explain a higher power, because I felt it. It just was and it just is. There was nowhere to go. No one to become. I was exactly where I needed to be. I gave all my trust to this infinite intelligence and surrendered to the fact that I was being guided by something much greater than myself. I embraced being one expression of the whole, and all the pressure of "figuring it out" dissolved. It was time to just be with what was.

WHAT YOU CAN CONTROL

Over the following year, I continued to integrate my lessons and began to hone my skills as a mental alchemist. Understanding I was connected to the oneness gave me this visceral knowing that the only thing holding me back from achieving anything I wanted from life was my own mental roadblocks in the form of self-limiting programming. I had this clear roadmap to success. All I needed to do was continue to transmute my programming to work for me, instead of against me, and I would create the outcomes I desired. Life became very simple. The only things in my control were my focus and choices. Through those two mechanisms, I could direct the entirety of my human experience.

Focus.

My conscious focus in the present moment and the subconscious focus, which is running my life through subconscious beliefs beneath the conscious surface.

Choices.

Which, to be fair, are a byproduct of where I choose to focus.

Whatever I focus on is what I get.

When I focus on what I want, I get more of what I want.

When I focus on what I don't want, I get more of what I don't want.

If I overeat chips, soda, and doughnuts every day, I will get more fat on my body. If I eat the right amount of nourishing and healthy foods, I will create and maintain a lean body.

If I neglect my family and friends, I will feel lonely. If I spend quality time with my loved ones, I will feel deeply connected.

If I procrastinate and don't do the most important things in my business, it won't grow. If I work diligently on the most important tasks in my business, it will grow.

We all get this as a society, and this is where most of our collective energy is being directed. The thing we don't get is that the choices we make are a byproduct of our focus (consciously and subconsciously.) I'll give you an example. If someone values family over everything and says they want to make a million dollars, but they believe that making more money means sacrificing their relationships with their family, they will never do what's necessary to make a million dollars.

It's not because they are unable to take the necessary actions to make a million dollars. It is because their subconscious will delete, generalize, or distort any information that would put them on the path to getting the million dollars. Conversely, if they believe they can make a million dollars while deepening their relationships with their family, they will do the necessary things to make a million dollars.

The subconscious has our survival as priority number one, so it doesn't matter how much you try to force things; it will continue to put up roadblocks until you change the underlying programming that threatens your survival. Again, none of this needs to be rational, and most of the time it isn't.

Is there a belief you are holding onto that may have kept you safe in the past but now needs to be released in order for you to step into the life you desire?

Speaking of a million dollars. Making a million dollars in my business was one of the clear outcomes I had for myself for years, and despite having traction in my business, I had never experienced the breakthrough success that would generate that type of revenue. It wasn't until I did an internal auditing of my beliefs around money that I discovered how much I was self-sabotaging my ability to get to this income level. No one in my family or friend group had ever made this much money, or anywhere near it, so my default subconscious beliefs were that it was impossible. This manifested in self-limiting beliefs.

It wasn't until I transmuted all these beliefs using their opposite polarity that the floodgates for money began to open up for me fully. (This process will happen for you in Part 2, Training 12.)

This looked like:

Old belief: I believe money is for rich people, and I am not a rich person.
New belief: I believe money is for me, and I am a rich person.

Old belief: I believe I don't deserve enough money to live comfortably.
New belief: I believe I deserve an abundance of money far beyond what is comfortable.

Old belief: I believe making money from something sacred like helping people is bad.
New belief: I believe making money from something sacred like helping people is good.

Old belief: I believe I am only making just enough money to get by.
New belief: I believe I am making way more money than is required to get by.

Old belief: I believe making lots of money is impossible.
New belief: I believe making lots of money is possible.

There were many more beliefs, but I will spare you a few pages of reading and stop there. Within six months of transmuting these beliefs, my business made $1.6 million dollars, and my take home of that was over $750,000. This was almost four times more money than I had ever made before.

Simultaneously, the income correlated with a massive growth in our online community. We built a YouTube channel with over a million subscribers and received over 100 million views from a community living in every pocket of the world.

Every outcome I desired was now exponentially coming to fruition through the power of aligning my subconscious programming to work for me, instead of against me. I was no longer forcing things. I was simply allowing myself to be who I was, and the money, followers, and prestige followed my frequency. I had accomplished more in those six months than I had in my previous seven years of hard work.

I repeated this process for all the areas of my life where I felt like I was living in lack. The result was attracting a whole new group of friends that sincerely wanted the best for me and were aligned with who I wanted to be.

I mended the relationship with my parents that had been tarnished ever since my core wound at seven years old, and I dealt with all my own self-limiting programming around romance, which led to a whole new depth of connection, love, and excitement between my wife and I.

Most importantly, I was now living in a state of peace. FINALLY. Peace. An empty mind. A state of equilibrium with my own mind and body. I had cleaned up all my core self-limiting beliefs around who I was, and my anxiety disappeared. I was at ease. I knew who I was, and I was ready to give my gifts to the world in the most authentic and joyful way I could imagine.

Reviewing the clear outcomes I had chosen for myself years earlier, I was now in complete alignment with the life I wanted to live. It was now time for me to take the final step where I would commit myself fully to my unique talent and what I intuitively knew was the path that would bring me the deepest fulfillment imaginable.

CHAPTER 16
LIVING YOUR TRUTH

W HEN YOU DO THE REQUIRED SUBCONSCIOUS reprogramming, you start to play an infinite game that aligns you with your unique talent and the ultimate experience of life. Every one of us has the opportunity to achieve amazing things and experience inner peace. Collectively as a species, we are deeply wounded emotionally, and if we want to step into a world we all want to live in, then it starts with reprogramming ourselves at the individual level. No longer can we sit idly by and hope that someone will save us. No one saved me. No one will save you. The only way we create heaven on earth is by committing to do the work on ourselves. One focus at a time. One choice at a time. We must own our own experience and trust that everything else will take care of itself.

THE UNIVERSE IS MENTAL

Although my fitness business was thriving, I knew that I needed to undergo another death and rebirth cycle to step into alignment with my fully embodied truth. Now that I had reached financial freedom with my business, I knew it was time to follow my intuition and get back to aligning once again with my unique talents. I had become this social media fitness influencer with millions of followers, and that identity was great for getting me to where I was, but it wasn't going to get me to where I wanted to go.

I began the process of transitioning out of my fitness business so I could pursue bringing this life-transforming reprogramming work to the world. Step by step I began firing myself from my operational tasks and replacing myself by hiring other people and implementing new systems to take my place. Doing so created the space to go deeper into my client work once again, so I could hone these skills I had used for myself and use them to support others. As I continued to clear my plate, more opportunities arose for me to work with clients and I began to step deeper into my most joyful work. You are now reading one of the most joyful pieces of work that I have created yet: my story and full playbook for personal transformation through subconscious reprogramming.

One thing that became apparent to me as I started this transition was that I had a maximal capacity, and to have the impact I wanted to have on the world, I needed to continue to remove things from my life that were interfering with my ability to do this transformational work at the highest level. As a practitioner, my ability to create transformation in others is only as good as the capacity I have for creating transformation within myself. The more space I create to transmute the programming within myself, the more capacity I have to facilitate transformation in my clients.

For example, I knew I needed to change my beliefs about how many clients I would have and, in general, how I would work with them. I needed to go from the paradigm of many clients at a surface level to a few clients at a deep level. I changed my beliefs to do this from:

"I believe I need lots of clients to be successful" to "I believe I need only a few of the right clients to be successful."

This belief gave me the bandwidth and permission to slow down and go to the depth necessary to bring the highest performers in the world to the next level of their game. (You will work on this in Part 2, Training 11.)

In perfect synchronicity, the more I let go of my old identity and way of being, the more opportunities arose for me to work with elite professional athletes, entrepreneurs, and other high performers. The more case studies I got under my belt, the better I got at teaching these modalities you are now reading about, and the more potent my coaching became.

After moving across the country with my family from Los Angeles, California, to Fort Lauderdale, Florida, I was now operating in a whole new energetic state. I had different people around me and was bringing in different types of opportunities. As another trophy to signify my graduation to this new season of life, I purchased my dream car: a brand new Mercedes Benz GLE 350 tricked out to the max. The reason I add that part in is because we get fed all these stories of what real inner peace looks like. Some people will tell you that it's the ability to let go of all worldly possessions, but to those people I would say they are missing the point. Inner peace is a baseline state of being that we work to maintain through our focus and choices every day. From that baseline, we have to recognize that we are playing an infinitely fun game, and anything that you feel enhances the experience of that game should be capitalized on—including a sick ass car! No, money won't bring you happiness or inner peace, but it sure as hell will enhance your experience of life if you have it.

The truth is that you can't compare your experience or desires to anyone else's. For me, a part of inner peace is living in financial abundance and surrounding myself with people, things, and experiences that make me feel held in this energetic frequency. Do I need this car? Fuck no. Is it super fun to drive, you bet!

BE THE PUREST ESSENCE

After moving to Florida, my confidence continued to grow, and I felt that I could transform the life of any high achiever that came across my path. One of the most full circle experiences was with my boxer who I had lost contact with years earlier when he had to cut off connection to pursue the reality TV show. One day I felt this strong impulse to reach out to him and decided, what the heck, I'll give him a call to see how he is doing. Upon getting on the call, he confessed to me that he was at the lowest of lows and was pleading with God to send him help.

Well, I guess that's my cue. Thanks for the nudge, God!

He had lost his last fight, which would have put him in a position for another world title fight, and he was deep in the pains of subconscious sabotage. He didn't lose the fight because he wasn't a good enough fighter. He lost because he didn't believe he was worthy of that level of success. Over the next few months, we went all in together and cleared out a tremendous amount of the programming that was still holding him back from being who he truly was.

By the time the fight week came around, he was the co-main event at the Alamo Bowl in a fight that would either put the nail in the coffin of his career or revive him. He was a big underdog in this fight, and no one gave him a chance outside of his own coaches. His opponent had already made it public that he was going to knock my fighter out cold. *Good,* I thought. This guy is in for a rude awakening. He has no idea the new fighter he was about to step into the ring with. Upon arriving at the fight a few days earlier for press days and weigh-ins, I could feel the purity in the energy of my fighter. He had no resistance. He was present. He was connected to something far greater than himself. Every few hours, we would go up to his hotel room to do some breathwork, and I would sit in front of him, auditing his energy for any impurities. Nothing could be found. He was ready. His time was now.

When fight night rolled around, there was an aura around the event that made it feel like we were living in a movie. My fighter is the son of a Hall of Fame boxer and really resonated with the story of Creed, because he was always told he shouldn't fight and was steered away from fighting earlier in his life. As I told you earlier, I had gotten into the world of boxing because I was inspired by the movie *Creed.* Not only that, but my fighter's cutman, the one who applies ice and works on the fighter between the rounds, was the same cutman they used in the *Creed* movies. And not only that, but the opponent was the same fighter they used as the actor who fought Creed in one of the movies.

You can't make this shit up! It was time for the show, and we began the ring walk.

Once we got to the ring, I took my seat ringside and sat back to watch the manifestation of our work together become reality for the world to see. From the opening bell, it was complete domination. Every time his opponent would lunge in for a big shot, my fighter would artfully counter him and make him pay. By the end of the fight, his opponent was attempting to draw him into a firefight in hopes of landing a lucky shot, but my fighter was too smart and locked in for that. In the past, he may have fallen for those tricks, but not tonight. He had nothing to prove to this guy. He knew who he was and was free to just fight his own fight. He used his skills to drown his opponent all the way through the final bell. It was a unanimous decision win, and from what I and the commentators saw was a complete shutout. I stormed the ring afterward as I embraced my fighter. He told me he loved me, and I told him I loved him. This was a fight for a secondary championship belt, but the real prize was the new reality my fighter had just stepped into. His rebirth had been completed, and he was now operating from a whole new identity. If he performed like that every night, there wasn't a fighter in his weight class that could beat him.

After the dust settled and I was back in my hotel room, I sat in contemplation of what we had just achieved together. What others thought was impossible was easy for us when the resistance was removed. What my fighter and I had accomplished together, you and I can accomplish as well.

THE JOURNEY NEVER ENDS

The truth is there are very few professional athletes and high performers in the world who do the work we are talking about here to remove the hidden resistance that puts into question who is going to show up in the moments that count the most. Each of us has our own stage in life to be our best, and there doesn't need to be a question of what version of ourselves will show up. The version of ourselves that is in flow and being our best is the only thing that remains when you remove the self-limiting programming that holds us back.

There is only one you. You are the person you need to be, and there is no one you need to be like or become. You, in your purest essence, free from the self-limiting programming, is all you need to be to perform your best.

The more I embrace this in my own life, the more it rings true. In my first year transitioning to a full-time mental performance coach, I completely replaced my salary from my previous business. Present day, I am fully transitioned out of my fitness business and have made my exit with enough money to sustain my family for years to come. Many people in my position would think it's crazy to give up such a profitable and peaking business when I did, but my intuition knew better than what other people could tell me. I knew that there was a death and rebirth that could only happen when I completely cut ties with my old identity and fully stepped into this new one that feels in full alignment with my true nature. Additionally, as I made this transition, I took all my own medicine that I am now sharing with you to make this process as easy and amicable as possible. You better believe that I had a whole list of self-limiting beliefs that were trying to hold me back from exiting the company and living my truth.

I believed that if I left my fitness business, I would never be successful on my own.

I believed that if I left my fitness business, everyone would hate me.

I believed that if I left my fitness business, I would lose all my friendships at that business.

There were so many more, but I did the same process I am sharing with you. One by one, I accepted that those beliefs were true, sat in them, grieved them fully, and then surrendered them. Then I chose the opposite polarity of each belief, which looked like this:

Old belief: I believe that if I leave my fitness business, I will never be successful on my own.

New belief: I believe that when I leave my fitness business, I will be successful on my own.

Old belief: I believe that if I leave my fitness business, everyone will hate me.

New belief: I believe that when I leave my fitness business, the right people will still love me.

Old belief: I believe that if I leave my fitness business. I will lose all my friendships at that business.

New belief: I believe that when I leave my fitness business, I will keep my friendships at that business that are meant to last.

This is just a sample of the work I am constantly doing within my own inner planet to move me toward becoming the man I want to be. One thing I want to drive home as I move you into the actionable training is that there is a lot of heavy lifting upfront to clean up your inner planet, but after a while, you will be mostly operating in a place of flow and synchronicity. Once your beliefs are in alignment with who you want to be, you will organically flow toward the life that is meant for you without needing to control as much of the process.

This way of living allows you to surrender the future and focus all your energy toward fully making the most out of what's in your control in the present moment. If you do that, you graduate onto playing an infinite game that becomes more and more joyful the more you let go and allow life to provide you with what's best for you. Oftentimes, what we receive when we are living in this aligned state is better than anything we could have hoped for. Speaking from experience, I've had everyone from MLB, to NFL, to MMA fighters referred to me within the past months without doing anything at all to attract their attention. The right people are showing up in my life to receive my support at the right time. I've also been blessed to work with a variety of business owners, executives, and other creators striving for greatness. Most importantly, I get to now take these skills and pass them down to my children. Looking into the eyes of my two-year-old daughter, I know that she is presently receiving her programming directly from how I am showing up in the world. Undoubtedly, there are still areas of growth, and I am striving to be better every day, but by my breaking the generational curses of those who came before me, she has the opportunity to be the absolute best version of herself.

The reason I wrote this book is to take you on my journey to a place I never thought imaginable before I began doing the subconscious reprogramming I have shared within my story. I was fighting an uphill battle my whole life until I learned how to align myself with the subconscious beliefs that eventually propelled me into my dream life. I trust that my story and personal playbook have found you at the right time in your life. Now the only thing left is for you to graduate onto Part 2 and start taking action. Yeah, I get it. There will inevitably still be the voice in the back of your head that says, "Will this really work for me, and will it be worth it?" Whenever I hear this voice, I say, "Go fuck yourself." And then I take the necessary action that lies ahead of me. I recommend you do the same and dive right into Part 2 of this book. It's been my greatest honor to share a little of my story with you. Now, let's get to work!

60 SECONDS TO CHANGE SOMEONE'S LIFE!

Have you heard of the law of cause and effect?

Often described as **Karma**...

Essentially, whatever energy you are projecting into the universe will inevitably come back to you in some shape or form.

You've experienced this many times before.

You hold the door for someone, you give a compliment, you do a random act of kindness *and* even if you don't receive direct physical compensation for this action, you receive the emotional reward of feeling good.

Which, at the end of the day, is what we are all looking for.

With that being said, I have a request for a random act of kindness :)

I wrote this book and it seems to be really impacting people's lives in a profound way. The problem is that 99.9999999% of people will never see this book if it doesn't get enough reviews on Amazon to make it visible in their rankings.

Since I am a self-published author, I am entirely reliant on you (my community of friends, acquaintances and readers) to get this book out into the world, so I can empower more people to program themselves to succeed.

If you can **leave me a review on Amazon,** this one action (that takes 60 seconds) will send waves of powerful positive energy into the universe that is destined to come back to you.

Not only that, but your review will help...

...one more person defeat the demons that cause anxiety/depression.

...one more person feel like they are not alone.

...one more person identify their unique talent.

...one more person believe in themselves.

...one more person feel like they are enough.

If you can take 60 seconds right now to leave a review, you will be sending waves of goodness into the world and I will personally be extremely grateful. So grateful that if you take a screenshot of your review and email it to me *brandon@theowned.industries*, I will send you a couple gifts in return.

If you are on Audible—hit the three dots in the top right of your device, click rate & review, then leave your honest feedback and a star rating.

If you are on kindle or an e-reader—you can scroll to the bottom of the book then swipe up and it will automatically prompt a review.

If you are reading the physical book—go to the book page on Amazon (search "Programmed to Fail") and then scroll down the page to leave a review.

Thank you so much for your support.

Now is the time for you to dive back in to take action in
Part 2: The Playbook.

Lots of love,
Brandon

PART 2

THE PLAYBOOK

Now that you know where this playbook came from, it's time to use your inspiration to put it into practice. Follow along step by step, and you will begin to master your inner world.

To be clear, this is not therapy or your typical personal development. This is an incremental program that, if followed step by step, will build upon itself and help you align all your programming with the outcomes you are striving toward. Ultimately, we are talking about playing an infinite game of life that you love. A game that is full of joy, connection, and purpose. There are no shortcuts, though. You have to do the work.

Some people work well with accountability, so you can build personal accountability by deciding on a consequence for yourself if you fall off the wagon—or you can find an accountability partner in the owned training community. Either way, you need to find a way to stay consistent. I personally like to schedule everything into my calendar to get it done. Maybe you create a recurring weekly event for yourself to come back to this training. Up to you!

While going through this playbook and doing the exercises, I recommend that you listen to binaural beats or any soothing meditation music throughout. It will help you decrease your brainwave frequencies, making it easier for you to turn off your thinking mind, so you can connect to your feeling body. Search your favorite music player like Spotify for "binaural beats" and you'll see plenty of options to choose from.

Additionally, if you would like to get video modules and coaching from me to get through this, check out www.theowned.industries/training where you can join my online class.

Let's begin.

TRAINING 1

SET YOUR INTENTION AND YOUR BASELINE

SET YOUR INTENTION

You're not going to do the work required to get through this playbook unless you have a driving force behind you.

What outcome would make going through this training worth all the time spent?

Imagine yourself three to six months from now after completing this.

Who would you be? What would you be able to achieve? Pick an intention for doing this training that will make it juicy for you.

Intention: ....

I recommend creating a Word document where you can track your progress and do this work with me, or if you have the physical copy, write directly into this book. Now that you have your intention set, let's get to work.

TODAY'S BASELINE

First things first, we need to establish where you are today as you start this journey. This isn't about judging yourself; it's about awareness. Just feel into this exercise, observe, and document what comes up.

Let's start with how it feels to be you right now. Close your eyes and turn off your thinking mind. Feel into your body without expectation and ask yourself, *How does it feel to be me right now?*

Sit into this question and feel the emotions that come up. Take your time. Write them down without judgment and then give your perceived state of being a score from 1 (the worst you could feel) to 10 (the best you could feel.)

Write the feelings that come up for you:

....

Give yourself a score from 1–10 *(1 being the worst and 10 being the best).*

1 2 3 4 5 6 7 8 9 10

The key is to not compare yourself to anything or anyone. Just feel what number is most true for you right now.

Now that you have documented your present state of being, you have the foundation for everything we will be doing going forward.

Everything we do in life is for a feeling.

We want more money for the feelings of freedom, security, and abundance.

We want a romantic relationship to feel love and connection.

We want success in our careers to feel purposeful.

That is why our feeling experience is the most important metric we have.

MAJOR LIFE AREA BASELINES

Now that you know what it feels like to be you right now, let's bring this same feeling exercise into the major areas of your life.

Write down how you feel from 1 (the worst) to 10 (the best) in regard to each of these areas of your life. Don't compare this to anyone else. This is strictly about how you feel in relation to each of these areas.

PHYSICAL HEALTH

Close your eyes and feel where your physical health is from 1–10 and document your answer.

If 1 would be your health is so bad that you are knocking on death's door and 10 is peak physical health and vitality for you personally, where would you land?

Give yourself a score from 1–10 *(1 being the worst and 10 being the best).*

1 2 3 4 5 6 7 8 9 10

MENTAL HEALTH (PEACE OF MIND)

Close your eyes and feel where your mental health is from 1–10 and document your answer.

If 1 is wanting to commit suicide and 10 is you are blissed out and feeling your very best, where would you land? This, of course, is generally speaking since emotions will always fluctuate. You are just giving yourself a score to best represent how you usually feel.

Give yourself a score from 1–10 *(1 being the worst and 10 being the best).*

1 2 3 4 5 6 7 8 9 10

CAREER (PURPOSEFUL WORK)

Close your eyes and feel your level of satisfaction with your career from 1–10 and document your answer.

If 1 equals you hate your work and it's the worst thing ever and 10 is you feel purposeful and get great joy from the work you do, where would you land?

Give yourself a score from 1–10 *(1 being the worst and 10 being the best).*

1 2 3 4 5 6 7 8 9 10

FINANCES

Close your eyes and feel your level of satisfaction with your finances from 1–10 and document your answer.

If 1 is you can't pay for your next meal and 10 is you have enough money to do everything you need and want to do in life, where do you land?

Give yourself a score from 1–10 *(1 being the worst and 10 being the best).*

1 2 3 4 5 6 7 8 9 10

TRIBE RELATIONSHIPS (CLOSE FRIENDS AND LOVED ONES)

There are a few categories for relationships, so give yourself three separate scores.

Close your eyes and feel your level of satisfaction with your tribe from 1–10 and document your answer.

Your tribe is your inner circle of friends, family, and loved ones that have your back no matter what. If you feel like no one cares about you, and you have no one to support you, then you are leaning toward a 1. If you feel like you are deeply supported and cared for by a close circle of people and it couldn't be any better, then give yourself a 10. Most of us fall somewhere in between.

Give yourself a score from 1–10 *(1 being the worst and 10 being the best).*

1 2 3 4 5 6 7 8 9 10

ROMANTIC RELATIONSHIP

Close your eyes and feel your level of satisfaction with your romantic relationship from 1–10 and document your answer.

Your romantic relationship is one that you are so intertwined with that if this isn't good, it can blow everything else up in your life. Give yourself a 1 if you are ready to break up and ranging to a 10 if you couldn't be happier with this relationship. If you are single right now, give yourself a score as it relates to your satisfaction with your current dating life.

Give yourself a score from 1–10 *(1 being the worst and 10 being the best).*

1 2 3 4 5 6 7 8 9 10

WORK RELATIONSHIPS

Close your eyes and feel your level of satisfaction with your work relationships from 1–10 and document your answer.

Your work relationships can range from a 1 (you hate working with every one of those assholes) to 10 (you couldn't be happier with your work relationships). Where do you land on this scale?

Take all the time you need to give yourself a solid baseline, and then let's move right into your training.

Give yourself a score from 1–10 *(1 being the worst and 10 being the best).*

1 2 3 4 5 6 7 8 9 10

TRAINING 2
EGO DEATH

B EFORE EMBARKING ON THIS JOURNEY OF uncovering who you are
now so you can step into who you have the capacity to become, I
want to once again mention an experience that was incredibly
valuable to me and something that is the first of two bonus/optional
training segments for you. As you read, the ego-death experience I had
using chemical compound 5-MeO-DMT (in my case, The Toad) was
crucial for creating the space to see my subconscious programming
without necessarily identifying with it. This was so impactful for me
because I had never before in my life been able to remove myself from
my identity. Once I had that experience, I could view my subconscious
programming more matter-of-factly instead of being so attached to it.
I could now see the programming that was working for me and the
programming that was working against me. Before that, I was blind to
it. After an ego-death experience, you are also in a very malleable state,
so it becomes much easier to change subconscious programming that
previously seemed impossible to remove.

Additionally, any ego-death experience separates you from your
identity and connects to the source of all that was, is, and will be. A
real visceral experience of what many people refer to as God. This
experience is incredibly empowering because it takes the pressure off
of you. It allows you to see yourself as a vessel for this infinite intelligence instead of feeling like you are alone trying to figure everything
out by yourself.

With that being said, if you are feeling called to facilitate an ego-death experience, it should not be taken lightly. You must be under the supervision of someone who ideally has decades of experience guiding people through their ego death. You also want to make sure you have a buffer around this experience where there are no expectations (work or otherwise) placed upon you for at least a week afterward.

I will explicitly say I am not recommending you undergo an ego death, but I am looking to empower those of you who have been seeking an experience like this to heed the call if you hear it. If you are being called to this experience it will be a feeling of deep knowing inside of you. It will be undeniable. You will feel fear and hesitancy about undergoing the experience, but a part of you will know that this is your destiny and you have no choice but to heed the call.

Finally, you can successfully do my training and reprogram your subconscious without an ego-death experience. In fact, most of my one-on-one clients have never experienced an ego death. If, however, you know that this will be valuable for you, there are many tools to make this happen. My preference for facilitating this experience is through 5-MeO-DMT, because it only lasts fifteen minutes but has a profound impact that will change you for the rest of your life. Now that I have spoken my truth on this topic, you can proceed with the rest of this training. Feel free to do the training in its entirety, and then afterward you can always circle back to considering having an ego-death experience.

TRAINING 3
AWAKEN YOUR AWARENESS

Y OU HAVE ESTABLISHED YOUR BASELINE, AND it is time to begin your mental training. This first section of your training is all about awakening your awareness. The first stage of learning is always unconscious incompetence, which essentially means we don't know what we don't know. Well, the only way to know what is holding you back is by getting a deeper awareness of what it's like to be you throughout your day.

The way we will uncover this awareness is through a simple exercise where you set alarms to go off every three hours throughout the day for a week. You can set five alarms a day, and that is plenty. So 8:00 a.m., 11:00 a.m., 2:00 p.m., 5:00 p.m., and 8:00 p.m. would be an example of your alarms for the day.

When an alarm goes off, stop what you are doing, close your eyes, and ask yourself, "How does it feel to be me right now?" Then document the answer in your notes in the same place you did the initial baseline training or directly in this book.

The format should look something like this:

Nov. 17, 8:00 a.m.: I feel grateful

Nov. 17, 11:00 a.m.: I feel anxious

Nov. 17, 2:00 p.m.: I feel in flow working

Nov. 17, 5:00 p.m.: I feel overwhelmed

Nov. 17, 8:00 p.m.: I feel exhausted and peaceful

These, of course, are just random feelings to give you some examples. The key is not to think about your feelings. Instead, just feel your feelings and name the present emotion. This is not a place to journal about what's going on or explain your feelings. Just document the feeling as if you were an observational data scientist. View your feelings as a piece of data that does not need to be rationalized or fixed. It just is. Document and move on.

If at any point you miss an alarm, don't worry—just move on to the next one. If you miss an entire day, don't worry—just do your next alarm. This isn't about being perfect. We just want to pull out enough data in a given week for you to gain awareness of what the general experience of being you is like.

Open your phone right now and set recurring alarms for the next week.

Start this exercise today and continue documenting your feeling experience for the next week.

If at any point you find yourself struggling with consistency, remember why you are doing this. What is the big juicy outcome that you're going to get from doing this training? Keep your focus there. After a week has passed, come back to this book, and we will move on to the next level of training.

Have fun! See you next week.

Write how it feels to be you when the alarm goes off:

DAY 1: ALARM 1: ....

DAY 1: ALARM 2: ....

DAY 1: ALARM 3: ....

DAY 1: ALARM 4: ....

DAY 1: ALARM 5: ....

Day 2: Alarm 1: ....

Day 2: Alarm 2: ....

Day 2: Alarm 3: ....

Day 2: Alarm 4: ....

Day 2: Alarm 5: ....

Day 3: Alarm 1: ....

Day 3: Alarm 2: ....

Day 3: Alarm 3: ....

Day 3: Alarm 4: ....

Day 3: Alarm 5: ....

Day 4: Alarm 1: ....

Day 4: Alarm 2: ....

Day 4: Alarm 3: ....

Day 4: Alarm 4: ....

Day 4: Alarm 5: ....

Day 5: Alarm 1: ....

Day 5: Alarm 2: ....

Day 5: Alarm 3: ....

Day 5: Alarm 4: ....

Day 5: Alarm 5: ....

DAY 6: ALARM 1: ....

DAY 6: ALARM 2: ....

DAY 6: ALARM 3: ....

DAY 6: ALARM 4: ....

DAY 6: ALARM 5: ....

DAY 7: ALARM 1: ....

DAY 7: ALARM 2: ....

DAY 7: ALARM 3: ....

DAY 7: ALARM 4: ....

DAY 7: ALARM 5: ....

THE CONNECTION BETWEEN FOCUS AND FEELINGS

THIS PART OF YOUR TRAINING BUILDS upon our work from last week. Take a moment to review your notes from this past week of documenting your feelings and just observe without judgment what it's like to be you. Emotions can bubble up for all sorts of reasons, which is why we don't necessarily want to rationalize every emotion that we have. Conversely, we know that much of our feelings are being guided by our focus.

This week you will make the conscious connection between how your focus can contribute to your feelings both good and bad.

The more aware you become of this connection, the more power you gain in directing your focus with intention.

As I harped on throughout my story, what you focus on is what you get.

When you focus on what you want, you get more of what you want.

When you focus on what you don't want, you get more of what you don't want.

This is not about positive thinking. This is about focusing your mind in a way that keeps your energy directed toward what you want. Let go of viewing thoughts as good or bad and embrace the lens of "Is this what I want or is this what I don't want?"

When first starting this training, you will feel as if it's extremely difficult to control where you are focusing. Don't worry. Your focus is like a muscle. The more you train it, the better you get. Through this week's exercise, you will begin to see more clearly how you are contributing to the way you feel through your focus and how this impacts the quality of your life.

Resist the urge to fix anything as you go through this week's exercise. Trust me when I say this can be very challenging, but it will all be worth it in the end. Just observe and document.

Again, set the same alarms from last week to go off every three hours and ask yourself the same question: "How does it feel to be me right now?" Upon documenting your feeling, I then want you to ask yourself, "What was I focused on in that split second before the feeling emerged?"

Here is an example of what this might look like:

Nov. 18, 8:00 a.m.:
- Feeling grateful
- Focused on how I got a great night's sleep and am excited for the day's events that lie ahead

Nov. 18, 11:00 a.m.:
- Feeling anxious
- Focused on how I have an upcoming meeting that could result in conflict

Nov. 18, 2:00 p.m.:
- Feeling in flow
- Focused on the work task at hand and getting it done to the best of my ability

Nov. 18, 5:00 p.m.:
- Feeling overwhelmed
- Focused on how I don't have enough time to get done with everything on my task list

Nov. 18, 8:00 p.m.:
- Feeling exhausted and peaceful
- Focused on resting and unwinding from a hard day's work

Again, these are just examples of what focus could be creating your feelings. Sometimes there may not be a connection between your conscious focus and your feelings, so just document both your feeling and focus like a data scientist. What was the feeling? Where was your focus?

There is no need to judge your experience, fix anything, or do anything at all. Just document and move on. Set your alarms now and do this for the next week. After you have collected your data, move on to the next section of training, where you will begin to experience some relief from emotions you don't like by learning to better direct your focus. That's for next week, though. This week surrender to the process and be the data scientist.

Write how it feels to be you and then what you were focused on right before the feeling emerged when the alarm goes off:

DAY 1: ALARM 1:
　Feeling ....
　Focus ....
DAY 1: ALARM 2:
　Feeling ....
　Focus ....
DAY 1: ALARM 3:
　Feeling ....
　Focus ....
DAY 1: ALARM 4:
　Feeling ....
　Focus ....
DAY 1: ALARM 5:
　Feeling ....
　Focus ....

DAY 2: ALARM 1:
  Feeling ....
  Focus ....

DAY 2: ALARM 2:
  Feeling ....
  Focus ....

DAY 2: ALARM 3:
  Feeling ....
  Focus ....

DAY 2: ALARM 4:
  Feeling ....
  Focus ....

DAY 2: ALARM 5:
  Feeling ....
  Focus ....

DAY 3: ALARM 1:
  Feeling ....
  Focus ....

DAY 3: ALARM 2:
  Feeling ....
  Focus ....

DAY 3: ALARM 3:
  Feeling ....
  Focus ....

DAY 3: ALARM 4:
  Feeling ....
  Focus ....

DAY 3: ALARM 5:
  Feeling ....
  Focus ....

DAY 4: ALARM 1:

Feeling

Focus

DAY 4: ALARM 2:

Feeling

Focus

DAY 4: ALARM 3:

Feeling

Focus

DAY 4: ALARM 4:

Feeling

Focus

DAY 4: ALARM 5:

Feeling

Focus

DAY 5: ALARM 1:

Feeling

Focus

DAY 5: ALARM 2:

Feeling

Focus

DAY 5: ALARM 3:

Feeling

Focus

DAY 5: ALARM 4:

Feeling

Focus

DAY 5: ALARM 5:

Feeling

Focus

DAY 6: ALARM 1:
Feeling ....
Focus ....

DAY 6: ALARM 2:
Feeling ....
Focus ....

DAY 6: ALARM 3:
Feeling ....
Focus ....

DAY 6: ALARM 4:
Feeling ....
Focus ....

DAY 6: ALARM 5:
Feeling ....
Focus ....

DAY 7: ALARM 1:
Feeling ....
Focus ....

DAY 7: ALARM 2:
Feeling ....
Focus ....

DAY 7: ALARM 3:
Feeling ....
Focus ....

DAY 7: ALARM 4:
Feeling ....
Focus ....

DAY 7: ALARM 5:
Feeling ....
Focus ....

TRAINING 5
REWIRING YOUR FOCUS TO GET WHAT YOU WANT

THIS PAST WEEK, YOU BEGAN THE process of going from unconscious incompetence to conscious competence. Review your notes and observe how your focus was contributing to your feelings. Notice how when you are focused on things you want to change in the future or the past, it can make you feel bad. Notice how when you were focused on what you wanted or were just present to life as it was unfolding, you felt better. Again, observe without judgment.

This week you start building mental muscle. Like any workout program, when you get started, you feel weak and struggle. The more you do it, the stronger you get and the easier it becomes.

Set the same alarms you have set in the past couple of weeks. This time around, when you notice yourself feeling bad, identify the focus that is making you feel bad and then flip it. Once you flip it, document the new feeling that emerges. You are not choosing the feeling. You are documenting what feeling emerges when you change your focus. If you notice you are feeling good, there is nothing to fix. Just document your feelings and focus and move on.

When you are focused on what you don't want, the opposite focus is what you do want.

The more you intentionally flip your focus, the more your subconscious mind will pick up on this pattern and begin to automatically flip it for you.

Again, I will reiterate this is not about positive or negative thinking. We are going beyond that paradigm. This is about focusing on what you want and not focusing on what you don't want.

You are a vessel that energy is flowing through, and your focus is the way that you direct that energy. The purpose of this exercise is to get you consistently directing that energy in a way that is in your best interest—working for you, instead of against you.

Here is an example of what this may look like:

Nov. 18, 8:00 a.m.:
- Feeling grateful
- Focused on how I got a great night's sleep and am excited for the day's events that lie ahead

Nov. 18, 11:00 a.m.:
- Feeling anxious
- Focused on how I have an upcoming meeting that could result in conflict
- New focus is how I am grateful for this upcoming meeting to get to a place of resolution
- New feeling is gratitude and excitement

Nov. 18, 2:00 p.m.:
- Feeling in flow
- Focused on the work task at hand and getting it done to the best of my ability

Nov. 18, 5:00 p.m.:
- Feeling overwhelmed
- Focused on how I don't have enough time to get done with everything on my task list
- New focus is how hard I worked and how much I have accomplished today
- New feeling is pride

Nov. 18, 8:00 p.m.:

- Feeling exhausted and peaceful
- Focused on resting and unwinding from a hard day's work

I will say this again for repetition's sake: You are only flipping your focus if you aren't feeling good and notice that your focus is contributing to that not feeling good. Once your new focus is documented and your mind is focused there, just document the feeling that emerges from your new chosen focus.

Set your alarms, have fun, and remember that what you focus on is what you get.

Write how it feels to be you and then what you were focused on right before the feeling emerged when the alarm goes off. If you are feeling bad, flip your focus (the opposite) and write down both the new focus and the new feeling that emerges following your new focus.

DAY 1: ALARM 1:
Feeling..
Focus...
New Focus (if necessary)...
New feeling (if necessary)...
DAY 1: ALARM 2:
Feeling..
Focus...
New Focus (if necessary)...
New feeling (if necessary)...
DAY 1: ALARM 3:
Feeling..
Focus...
New Focus (if necessary)...
New feeling (if necessary)...

DAY 1: ALARM 4:

Feeling ....

Focus ....

New Focus (if necessary)...

New feeling (if necessary)..

DAY 1: ALARM 5:

Feeling ....

Focus ....

New Focus (if necessary)...

New feeling (if necessary)..

DAY 2: ALARM 1:

Feeling ....

Focus ....

New Focus (if necessary)...

New feeling (if necessary)..

DAY 2: ALARM 2:

Feeling ....

Focus ....

New Focus (if necessary)...

New feeling (if necessary)..

DAY 2: ALARM 3:

Feeling ....

Focus ....

New Focus (if necessary)...

New feeling (if necessary)..

DAY 2: ALARM 4:

Feeling ....

Focus ....

New Focus (if necessary)...

New feeling (if necessary)..

DAY 2: ALARM 5:
Feeling
Focus
New Focus (if necessary)
New feeling (if necessary)

DAY 3: ALARM 1:
Feeling
Focus
New Focus (if necessary)
New feeling (if necessary)
DAY 3: ALARM 2:
Feeling
Focus
New Focus (if necessary)
New feeling (if necessary)
DAY 3: ALARM 3:
Feeling
Focus
New Focus (if necessary)
New feeling (if necessary)
DAY 3: ALARM 4:
Feeling
Focus
New Focus (if necessary)
New feeling (if necessary)
DAY 3: ALARM 5:
Feeling
Focus
New Focus (if necessary)
New feeling (if necessary)

DAY 4: ALARM 1:

Feeling ....

Focus ....

New Focus (if necessary)...

New feeling (if necessary)..

DAY 4: ALARM 2:

Feeling ....

Focus ....

New Focus (if necessary)...

New feeling (if necessary)..

DAY 4: ALARM 3:

Feeling ....

Focus ....

New Focus (if necessary)...

New feeling (if necessary)..

DAY 4: ALARM 4:

Feeling ....

Focus ....

New Focus (if necessary)...

New feeling (if necessary)..

DAY 4: ALARM 5:

Feeling ....

Focus ....

New Focus (if necessary)...

New feeling (if necessary)..

DAY 5: ALARM 1:

Feeling ....

Focus ....

New Focus (if necessary)...

New feeling (if necessary)..

DAY 5: ALARM 2:

Feeling

Focus

New Focus (if necessary)

New feeling (if necessary)

DAY 5: ALARM 3:

Feeling

Focus

New Focus (if necessary)

New feeling (if necessary)

DAY 5: ALARM 4:

Feeling

Focus

New Focus (if necessary)

New feeling (if necessary)

DAY 5: ALARM 5:

Feeling

Focus

New Focus (if necessary)

New feeling (if necessary)

DAY 6: ALARM 1:

Feeling

Focus

New Focus (if necessary)

New feeling (if necessary)

DAY 6: ALARM 2:

Feeling

Focus

New Focus (if necessary)

New feeling (if necessary)

DAY 6: ALARM 3:

Feeling ....

Focus ....

New Focus (if necessary)..

New feeling (if necessary)...

DAY 6: ALARM 4:

Feeling ....

Focus ....

New Focus (if necessary)..

New feeling (if necessary)...

DAY 6: ALARM 5:

Feeling ....

Focus ....

New Focus (if necessary)..

New feeling (if necessary)...

DAY 7: ALARM 1:

Feeling ....

Focus ....

New Focus (if necessary)..

New feeling (if necessary)...

DAY 7: ALARM 2:

Feeling ....

Focus ....

New Focus (if necessary)..

New feeling (if necessary)...

DAY 7: ALARM 3:

Feeling ....

Focus ....

New Focus (if necessary)..

New feeling (if necessary)...

DAY 7: ALARM 4:
Feeling ....
Focus ....
New Focus (if necessary) ....
New feeling (if necessary) ....
DAY 7: ALARM 5:
Feeling ....
Focus ....
New Focus (if necessary) ....
New feeling (if necessary) ....

TRAINING 6
ELIMINATE WHAT NO LONGER SERVES YOU

C ONGRATULATIONS ON MAKING IT THROUGH THE conscious section of rewiring your focus. Take out your notes and observe how flipping your focus impacted your feelings. After you have reviewed your notes, like a good data scientist, ask yourself, "What are the glaring negative patterns, behaviors, or environments that lead to you not feeling good?"

It's time for you to get to work, making some lifestyle changes based on what you learned.

What habits have you been participating in that make you feel bad?

Maybe it's the anxiety created when you binge-check your email inbox. Maybe it's the anger created when you check social media. Maybe it's the apathetic feeling when you hang out with certain people. It's time to detox your mind by eliminating what's no longer serving you.

One thing I often recommend at this stage of your training is a media detox. Since you are going deeper into understanding yourself, it only makes sense to start to block out all the voices from other people who may be getting into your head.

Try abstaining from social media, the news, and any other consumption of information this week (good or bad) to see how removing it impacts your life.

At this stage, you are not adding anything new. You may identify that you feel better when doing certain things versus other things. As we advance in this training, you will add more to your plate that will make you feel better. At this stage, we are only removing things from your plate.

Identify the behaviors, environments, things you consume, and anything else that you have observed contributes to your not feeling your best, and either limit or remove those things altogether for the next week.

Some examples of this might be:

- No more snacking after dinner
- No more coffee in the afternoon
- No more social media on my phone
- No more gossiping about people
- No more email on my phone
- No more news apps on my phone or no more watching news
- Limit alcohol/smoking
- Limit TV time
- Eliminate or limit interactions with "x" person
- Eliminate or limit "x" environment from your weekly schedule

Some things will be outside of your control, and that's okay. Do your best to detox everything that is in your control.

Finally, once you have your game plan in place in regard to what will be limited or removed, you can come back to observe how you feel in your final week of alarms.

You will set the alarms just like you did last week and do the exact same exercise as you did last week. The only difference is you are doing it while also eliminating or limiting what you have observed contributes to your not feeling good.

Create your detox game plan, set your alarms, and have a great week ahead!

DETOX GAMEPLAN (LIST WHAT YOU WILL ELIMINATE OR LIMIT)

....

....

....

....

....

....

....

....

....

....

....

....

....

Write how it feels to be you and then what you were focused on right before the feeling emerged when the alarm goes off. If you are feeling bad, flip your focus (the opposite) and write down both the new focus and the new feeling that emerges following your new focus.

DAY 1: ALARM 1:

Feeling...

Focus..

New Focus (if necessary)...

New feeling (if necessary)..

DAY 1: ALARM 2:

Feeling...

Focus..

New Focus (if necessary)...

New feeling (if necessary)..

DAY 1: ALARM 3:

Feeling...

Focus...

New Focus (if necessary)...

New feeling (if necessary)...

DAY 1: ALARM 4:

Feeling...

Focus...

New Focus (if necessary)...

New feeling (if necessary)...

DAY 1: ALARM 5:

Feeling...

Focus...

New Focus (if necessary)...

New feeling (if necessary)...

DAY 2: ALARM 1:

Feeling...

Focus...

New Focus (if necessary)...

New feeling (if necessary)...

DAY 2: ALARM 2:

Feeling...

Focus...

New Focus (if necessary)...

New feeling (if necessary)...

DAY 2: ALARM 3:

Feeling...

Focus...

New Focus (if necessary)...

New feeling (if necessary)...

DAY 2: ALARM 4:

Feeling ....

Focus ....

New Focus (if necessary) ....

New feeling (if necessary) ....

DAY 2: ALARM 5:

Feeling ....

Focus ....

New Focus (if necessary) ....

New feeling (if necessary) ....

DAY 3: ALARM 1:

Feeling ....

Focus ....

New Focus (if necessary) ....

New feeling (if necessary) ....

DAY 3: ALARM 2:

Feeling ....

Focus ....

New Focus (if necessary) ....

New feeling (if necessary) ....

DAY 3: ALARM 3:

Feeling ....

Focus ....

New Focus (if necessary) ....

New feeling (if necessary) ....

DAY 3: ALARM 4:

Feeling ....

Focus ....

New Focus (if necessary) ....

New feeling (if necessary) ....

DAY 3: ALARM 5:

Feeling ....

Focus ....

New Focus (if necessary) ....

New feeling (if necessary) ....

DAY 4: ALARM 1:

Feeling ....

Focus ....

New Focus (if necessary) ....

New feeling (if necessary) ....

DAY 4: ALARM 2:

Feeling ....

Focus ....

New Focus (if necessary) ....

New feeling (if necessary) ....

DAY 4: ALARM 3:

Feeling ....

Focus ....

New Focus (if necessary) ....

New feeling (if necessary) ....

DAY 4: ALARM 4:

Feeling ....

Focus ....

New Focus (if necessary) ....

New feeling (if necessary) ....

DAY 4: ALARM 5:

Feeling ....

Focus ....

New Focus (if necessary) ....

New feeling (if necessary) ....

DAY 5: ALARM 1:

Feeling

Focus

New Focus (if necessary)

New feeling (if necessary)

DAY 5: ALARM 2:

Feeling

Focus

New Focus (if necessary)

New feeling (if necessary)

DAY 5: ALARM 3:

Feeling

Focus

New Focus (if necessary)

New feeling (if necessary)

DAY 5: ALARM 4:

Feeling

Focus

New Focus (if necessary)

New feeling (if necessary)

DAY 5: ALARM 5:

Feeling

Focus

New Focus (if necessary)

New feeling (if necessary)

DAY 6: ALARM 1:

Feeling

Focus

New Focus (if necessary)

New feeling (if necessary)

DAY 6: ALARM 2:

Feeling ....

Focus ....

New Focus (if necessary)...

New feeling (if necessary)..

DAY 6: ALARM 3:

Feeling ....

Focus ....

New Focus (if necessary)...

New feeling (if necessary)..

DAY 6: ALARM 4:

Feeling ....

Focus ....

New Focus (if necessary)...

New feeling (if necessary)..

DAY 6: ALARM 5:

Feeling ....

Focus ....

New Focus (if necessary)...

New feeling (if necessary)..

DAY 7: ALARM 1:

Feeling ....

Focus ....

New Focus (if necessary)...

New feeling (if necessary)..

DAY 7: ALARM 2:

Feeling ....

Focus ....

New Focus (if necessary)...

New feeling (if necessary)..

DAY 7: ALARM 3:

Feeling ....

Focus ....

New Focus (if necessary) ....

New feeling (if necessary) ....

DAY 7: ALARM 4:

Feeling ....

Focus ....

New Focus (if necessary) ....

New feeling (if necessary) ....

DAY 7: ALARM 5:

Feeling ....

Focus ....

New Focus (if necessary) ....

New feeling (if necessary) ....

TRAINING 7

IDENTIFYING YOUR UNIQUE TALENT

BONUS SECTION! THIS IS THE SECOND section in this training, which is not mandatory but highly recommended. In this section, you will identify your unique talent if you haven't already done so. Before we step into the next section, where you will be crafting your vision for your life, you want to identify what unique talent you have that will be the rocket fuel to get you to that vision.

Your unique talent is an intersection between what you are good at, what you enjoy most, and what can contribute to something greater than yourself. You do those three things, and your unique talent will bring you all the money you need to live a good life.

If you already are clear on what your unique talent is, jump ahead to the next level of training.

If you are unclear, try these lists:

LIST 1: JOYS

List one should be an emptying out of everything you enjoy no matter whether you think it's monetizable or not. If you like watching movies, then write that down. If you like riding your bike, then write that down. If you enjoy collecting baseball cards, write that down. If you like working out, then write that down. Literally, write down everything you enjoy, and have fun with this.

....

....

....

....

....

....

....

....

....

....

....

....

....

LIST 2: STRENGTHS

List number two should be separate from list number one and should include everything you feel you are either good at now or are willing to work to be good at in the future. This could be making sales calls. It could be writing. It could be networking. Let it rip! Everything you are good at or willing to commit to being good at should be on this list.

....

....

....

....

....

....

....

....

....

....

LIST 3: INTERSECTIONS

List number three is going to require you to first combine lists one and two. Create a third list, which includes all the things that intersect between what you enjoy and what you are good at. Since you probably aren't good at everything or willing to be good at everything, this third list should be shorter than the first two.

Here are some examples of what this might look like.

If you love sports and are also a lawyer, you can pursue a job at a sports agency.

If you love fitness and are really good at taking photos and making videos, you may want to find a way to join a team that creates media around wellness or do it through your own social media.

If you are really into anti-aging and you are a doctor, maybe you can explore a career as a functional medicine doctor that works in peak performance and anti-aging.

If you are really interested in fashion and also have design skills, maybe you can work for a clothing company or start your own fashion brand.

The key is to find that intersection between what you love and the skills you already possess or the skills you are willing to learn.

....

....

....

....

....

....

....

....

....

....

LIST 4: CONTRIBUTIONS

Finally, in list number four, identify what you can take from list three and utilize to contribute to something greater than yourself. This could be your ability to make sales calls to get a meaningful product or service to people who need it. This could be taking your passion for working out and helping people in your community create physical transformations. This could be taking your love for networking and using it to help someone grow their existing movement. Ultimately, we are talking about solving a problem or bringing value in some way that you would enjoy.

....

....

....

....

....

....

....

....

....

....

....

....

Once you have your fourth list, which only contains things that intersect between what you are good at, what you enjoy, and what contributes to something or someone greater than yourself, you are ready to harness your unique talent by choosing a path to pursue.

Don't put so much pressure on yourself to pick the right thing. The right thing right now may lead to a different thing in the future. Life is not linear, but it does reward you for aligning with your unique talents.

Pick one unique talent of yours that you would like to harness going forward, and I want you to keep that in mind when going into the next section of your training, where you will be stepping into the vision for your life. Surrender that you don't have it all figured out. Trust me, no one does. As you head into the next section just imagine how you would or could utilize this unique talent as a career path that fits into a compelling vision for your life.

If you identify that your unique talent is different from what you are currently doing, that is 100 percent okay. Trust that you are on a path to eventually get into alignment with this unique talent, and it doesn't need to happen overnight. The first step is simply staying curious and identifying what life might be like if you did pursue bringing your unique talent into the world.

After completing this exercise, hop right into the next level of training.

TRAINING 8
STEP INTO YOUR VISION

T AKE A MOMENT TO REVIEW YOUR notes from the past few weeks and observe how limiting or eliminating certain things from your routine has contributed to feeling better or worse. What would you like to continue with?

Decide for yourself what elimination or limitations would be in your best interest to continue and make that a part of your new lifestyle. Today the fun really begins, because you get to choose a compelling vision for your life.

You have two options for this.

If you are good at visualization, you can simply turn on your favorite relaxing music, close your eyes, and imagine what you would like your life to look and feel like one year from now.

If you would like a more guided visualization, go to my YouTube channel by searching "Brandon Epstein" and then go to the search bar within my channel and type in "Visualize Your Perfect Year." Listen to this meditation. You can also tap into the course here: www.theowned. industries/training, which contains additional listening materials.

Whatever option you choose, give yourself the time and space to do this exercise. Block off an entire hour to go deep into this world you will be stepping into.

The purpose of this exercise is to give your subconscious a clear GPS coordinate to start to move toward. There will undoubtedly be some resistance between where you are now and what you experience in the vision; let that be okay. Accept where you are, but begin to anchor yourself in this new reality through this exercise.

After you complete the visualization, write down a descriptive story of what you are experiencing in this vision for your future life. Write this story in the first person as if it is already true. Describe the detailed vision you are stepping into as if it were your reality right now. Again, write this in the same document that you have done all the previous exercises.

This might look something like this:

I wake up feeling refreshed, energized, and grateful in a comfortable bed next to the person I love most in a beautiful room that inspires me. Before getting out of bed, I bask in the gratitude of how far I have come on my journey and how excited I am for the day ahead. I start my morning slowly with a hot cup of coffee and some inventory of what's on my calendar for the day. I do some stretching and meditation to ground myself before getting into any work. After eating a nutritious breakfast that fills me up, but keeps me feeling light, I move into my favorite task of the day, which is working with one of my most inspiring clients. Etc.

Read this every morning when you wake up and every night before going to sleep for the next seven days.

Warning: you may have thoughts like, *How will this ever happen?* and *What can I do now?*

As I said at the outset, this is not fast food training. There is a proven process you are following. Don't start doing anything yet. You will have the rest of your life to start doing. Instead, just give yourself the gift every day of planting the seed for the life you are stepping into. You are familiarizing your subconscious with what your new normal will be.

Final warning: don't choose a vision that you think will make you happy because you saw someone else having "x" in their life and believe that will make you happy as well. This is all about you. Choose a vision that you believe will bring you the feeling experience you desire. It doesn't have to be anything crazy like I have a 100-million-dollar business that cures every disease and creates world peace. Be selfish with this and make it feel attainable and desirable, but still push your edge. As you play the infinite game of life, your consciousness will shift, and you will desire different things. That is okay. Start with a vision that feels compelling to you right now.

Next week you will go to a greater place of clarity. This week is all about identifying what life you can step into to create the feeling experience you desire.

Write your vision here or put it in your own personal document:

....

....

....

....

....

....

....

....

....

....

....

....

....

....

....

....

....

....

....

CREATE CLARITY THROUGH CLEAR OUTCOMES

N OW THAT YOU HAVE A BIG juicy vision to work toward, let's chunk it
down and make it actionable.

Review your vision once again and identify the most compelling
outcomes within that vision and then write them out underneath your
vision with clarity.

REASSESS BASELINES

I advise you to start this process by returning to your baseline again and
seeing where you are now in the different areas of your life.

PHYSICAL HEALTH

Close your eyes and feel where your physical health is from 1–10 and
document your answer.

(the worst) **1 2 3 4 5 6 7 8 9 10** *(the best)*

MENTAL HEALTH (PEACE OF MIND)

Close your eyes and feel where your mental health is from 1–10 and
document your answer.

(the worst) **1 2 3 4 5 6 7 8 9 10** *(the best)*

CAREER (PURPOSEFUL WORK)

Close your eyes and feel your level of satisfaction with your career from 1–10 and document your answer.

(the worst) **1 2 3 4 5 6 7 8 9 10** *(the best)*

FINANCES

Close your eyes and feel your level of satisfaction with your finances from 1–10 and document your answer.

(the worst) **1 2 3 4 5 6 7 8 9 10** *(the best)*

TRIBE RELATIONSHIPS (CLOSE FRIENDS AND LOVED ONES)

Close your eyes and feel your level of satisfaction with your tribe from 1–10 and document your answer.

(the worst) **1 2 3 4 5 6 7 8 9 10** *(the best)*

ROMANTIC RELATIONSHIP

Close your eyes and feel your level of satisfaction with your romantic relationship from 1–10 and document your answer.

(the worst) **1 2 3 4 5 6 7 8 9 10** *(the best)*

WORK RELATIONSHIPS

Close your eyes and feel your level of satisfaction with your work relationships from 1–10 and document your answer.

(the worst) **1 2 3 4 5 6 7 8 9 10** *(the best)*

Give yourself new scores that represent where you feel you are now in each of the areas of your life by feeling into each category. It's okay if they haven't changed much, because we have yet to start the heavy lifting in regard to what will create the most tangible results in your life. Right now we are just checking in and bringing awareness to what it's like to be you in each of these areas right now.

IDENTIFY CLEAR OUTCOMES

Once you have established a new baseline, identify what clear, attainable outcomes would get you from where you are now to where you want to be in your vision.

An example of a clear outcome for my physical health is:

My physical health is the epitome of perfection as I have boundless energy, an impenetrable immune system, and I look and feel strong, lean, and youthful.

An example of a clear outcome for my finances is:

My finances are taken care of through my income that ranges from $30,000–$100,000 a month.

Some examples of clear outcomes for my career are:

- **My career is fulfilling as I get to go extremely deep with a handful of clients I coach.**
- **My career is extremely exciting as I get to travel around the world, speaking to new audiences and educating them on my teachings.**

Some examples of clear outcomes for my relationships are:

- **My friendships are deeply connected and keep me in alignment with the man I want to be while having enormous amounts of fun.**
- **My romantic relationship makes me feel loved and taken care of.**

- **Fatherhood is what connects me to my greatest purpose as I get to pass on an operating system to my children that removes all limitations for them and brings us all deep connection, love, and joy.**
- **My work relationships keep me engaged in the world in a way that connects me to a higher power and keeps me growing.**

An example of a clear outcome for my mental health is:

My mental space is a place of unique bliss. I love being with myself because of the beautiful inner planet I have designed for myself to live on.

As you can see, I am most interested in the way these outcomes will make me feel. It's not about the outcome really; it's about the feeling it will help align you with.

I have done this exercise for years, so I am a little more fluffy when it comes to my outcomes, but if this is the first time you are doing this, I recommend picking outcomes that will be obvious when you achieve them.

For example, you can say:

"I weigh 170 pounds."

"I have 'x' job."

"I work 'x' number of hours a week."

"I do 'x' fun activities every week."

"I go on 'x' dates each month to connect deeply with my partner."

Make these outcomes personal and meaningful for you. To make these feel highly attainable, write out only outcomes you believe you can achieve within a year from now—the same place you imagine yourself being when you read your vision.

Make each outcome as clear as possible and as actionable as possible.

You want to be able to clearly know when you have hit the target. This helps your subconscious come up with ideas and pathways for you to get to the said outcome.

Have fun with this, and once your outcomes are clearly documented, hop right into the next session, where we will begin to move you through any resistance that may be holding you back from getting to that outcome.

PHYSICAL HEALTH OUTCOME(S)

....

....

MENTAL HEALTH OUTCOME(S)

....

....

FINANCIAL OUTCOME(S)

....

....

CAREER OUTCOME(S)

....

....

TRIBE OUTCOME(S)

....

....

ROMANTIC RELATIONSHIP OUTCOME(S)

....

....

WORK RELATIONSHIPS OUTCOME(S)

....

....

ADDITIONAL LIFE OUTCOME(S)

....

....

....

....

TRAINING 10
UNCOVER YOUR SUBCONSCIOUS PROGRAMMING

IT IS TIME TO UNCOVER THE hidden resistance that has been holding you back from getting the feelings and experiences you desire most.

As I mentioned in my own story, you may have self-limiting programming that stems from your core wound. The good news is that you don't need to resolve your core wound to change the self-limiting programming created by this negative life experience. When you follow this training, the transmutation of your self-programming will resolve any corresponding issues you may have had from that core wound. Think about it this way. You had this scar tissue built up from this emotional injury. If we remove the scar tissue, we do not need to go back and reconcile what created it. The problem was never your core wound in itself. It was the self-limiting programming that was created by the core wound.

You ready for this?

PREPARE

We are going to start by having you identify what your foundational core beliefs are and how those beliefs are either pushing you toward your desired outcomes or pulling you away from them. Before hopping right into this exercise, make sure you are in a quiet and private place where you feel completely comfortable to let yourself have this experience without fearing judgment. If you'd like to do something ceremonial to make this feel even more intentional, light a candle before you begin.

Additionally, I recommend listening to binaural beats while doing this exercise to help drop your brainwaves down to a level where you can access your subconscious mind.

I would never recommend the use of illicit or illegal drugs, but if you are the type of person who benefits from a microdose of mushrooms, now would be the time to take no more than .1–.2 grams before starting this exercise.

What we are doing now is setting the stage for you to get past the conscious barriers that usually keep you stuck in your thinking mind. Thinking is not going to be useful for this exercise. We want to get to the subconscious supercomputer mind that holds onto your unconscious beliefs.

We are going to work with your beliefs because they are the pieces of code within your supercomputer that determine how you interrupt the world around you. It's not the external event that makes you feel bad or good. It's your own beliefs about the event that gives it meaning. This is why two people can look at the same president on TV and one can be filled with outrage and another can be filled with pride. It is you who gives the external events meaning, and you do so through your belief system.

Let's not label it good or bad as we go into this. Instead, just view it matter-of-factly as something that will push you toward your desired outcome or something that will hold you back from it.

Here it is. You create your reality in this way: you hear, smell, taste, touch, and see the world around you. That sensory experience runs down through your belief system, which gives it meaning, and then you consciously make an internal representation of this. That internal representation determines whether you want to go toward something or want to get away from something.

I will repeat myself in saying you didn't choose the beliefs you have, so don't make them wrong, don't beat yourself up for them, and don't feel bad if you find out you have self-limiting beliefs. As I shared in my personal story, I had hundreds of self-limiting beliefs, and the gift in them is that you can transmute them and reclaim that energy to work for you. That is why you can't think about these beliefs. Your thinking mind will play tricks on you. You need to feel where these beliefs live in your physical body. That means putting yourself in a relaxed state and feeling the emotions that come up within your physical body instead of thinking about them and creating stories around them. The feeling will reveal the subconscious belief, not your rational mind. If you would like me to guide you through this experience with more depth, definitely check out the course I made available at www.theowned.industries/training. You are ready for this. The previous training sessions have prepared you for the work we are now going to do together.

Relax and let's get started.

I BELIEVE I AM...

Write out the words "I believe I am," and then—without thinking, just feeling—write out what comes up for you. It may take seconds, or it may take minutes for the words to come through.

Keep feeling into your body and repeating "I believe I am" until something comes up.

As soon as something comes up, start writing down: I believe I am: COOL, an ASSHOLE, LOVING, STUPID—whatever comes up, don't judge it, just let it flow. As you write, try to leave space around each belief (this will make later training sessions easier).

Keep writing out what you believe about yourself until you start repeating yourself and feel like you have nothing else to say.

I believe I am ....

I believe I am ....

I believe I am ....

I believe I am ....

I believe I am ....

I believe I am ....

I believe I am ....

I believe I am ....

I believe I am ....

I believe I am ....

I believe I am ....

I BELIEVE PEOPLE ARE...

After you have done so, do the same thing for "I believe people are."

I believe people are SCARY, NEEDED, SELFISH, FUNNY—whatever comes up, don't judge it, just let it flow.

I believe people are ....

I believe people are ....

I believe people are ....

I believe people are ....

I believe people are ....

I BELIEVE THE WORLD IS...

Next up: "I believe the world is," and let it flow.

You can then think of any other areas of your life that are charged and may have self-limiting beliefs surrounding them, like money, relationships, your health, or anything else.

Once you have purged out all your beliefs about these things, exhale. Great job.

I believe the world is ....

I believe the world is ....

I believe the world is ....

I believe the world is ....

I believe the world is ....

EMOTIONS AND BELIEFS ABOUT YOUR OUTCOMES

We are now going to move into uncovering the self-limiting beliefs you may have in relation to the clear outcomes you have chosen for yourself in the last training. One by one choose the clear outcomes you have chosen, feel into the actions that may be required to get there, and then identify the emotions that come up within you.

If, for example, you feel into making a certain amount of money and a feeling of anxiety arises, then ask yourself what you believe to be true that would make you feel anxious about making that amount of money.

What's critical here is that when you feel the emotion (like anxiety) in your body, identify where exactly that emotion is in your physical body. Once you have done so, feel deeper and deeper into that physical location in your body and make that emotion stronger and stronger until something pops up when you ask yourself, "What am I believing to be true that would make me feel this way?"

Write down all the beliefs that come up.

An example for money might be "I believe I am not smart enough to make 'x' amount of money."

Whatever comes up, just write it down without judgment. After you have purged out all the beliefs that are creating resistance to one outcome, move on to the next and repeat the same exercise. Keep doing this until you have purged and documented all your foundational beliefs and all the beliefs that would interfere with your getting to your desired outcomes.

This is NOT fast food. Take your time. If you need multiple sessions to get through this, take all the time you need. There is no rush.

Once you have purged everything out and it's documented, you can move on to the next level of training, where you will process these uncovered beliefs.

Additional Beliefs

....

....

....

....

....

....

....

....

....

....

....

....

....

ACCEPT AND SURRENDER THE OLD YOU

DEEPLY HONOR YOU FOR GETTING THIS far. Uncovering what has been holding you back is a deeply uncomfortable process with little immediate gratification. If you enjoy uncovering your vulnerabilities like me, you may have gotten a thrill out of uncovering how much potential you have been leaving on the table due to poor programming. If you are more so just urgently ready to let that shit go, I understand you fully. Let's get into it.

You are now making the unconscious conscious. It's going to feel raw. Stick with me here.

Again, I recommend that you listen to some binaural beats or some sort of healing frequency audio to help you drop into your subconscious mind throughout this session. Bring up all the beliefs that you found from the previous session, and we will begin to release them through a process of acceptance and surrender. One by one, you must accept what is so that you can change it, and surrender what was so that you can move forward with new programming.

LABEL

In front of all your previous beliefs, write the words "Old belief:"

For example: "Old belief: I believe I am worthless."

ACCEPT

Then close your eyes and fully accept that you believe that about yourself right now, regardless of whether it is rationally true or not.

Take deep belly breaths and feel yourself receiving this belief without resistance. Just let it in so it can be heard and have its time in the sun before we let it go.

When you do this, you are removing the charge from the belief, and it loses its power over you. Hence the old saying, "What we resist, persists." Stop resisting, and it will stop persisting.

After fully accepting the belief and no longer trying to fight it or get away from it, you are ready to surrender it.

SURRENDER

I like to imagine my life on a timeline where everything that happens in the future is to the right, everything that happens in the past is to the left, and everything that is happening right now is presently right in front of me like a horse with blinders on.

Close your eyes and try to visualize this energetic timeline spread out in front of you.

Now bring the belief to mind that you want to change and feel all the negative emotions associated with believing this to be true. Imagine this belief is an energetic cloud full of these toxic emotions floating right in front of your face. See the colors, feel the emotions, and fully be with them.

Then I want you to breathe in deeply through your nose, and as you exhale, imagine a powerful wind blowing from right to left, blowing this belief into the past on your timeline. Visualize this belief moving to the left until it's in the past, and then watch it as it continues to go farther and farther into the past as you ground yourself deeper and deeper into the present.

Continue to breathe deeply through your belly as you watch that old belief become a distant story of the past. Watch the belief lose all its color, become translucent, and shrink down to the size of a grain of sand. Watch it go farther and farther into the past until you lose sight of this old belief in the distant horizon of the past.

Then bring your attention back to the present moment and experience the spaciousness of being free from this belief. Notice how much lighter you feel. Notice how much more relaxed you are. Notice how many more possibilities there are for you now.

Continue to breathe through the surrendering of this belief until you feel fully present and free from it. Take all the time you need to do this. There is no rush.

CONTINUE

Once you have fully released yourself from one belief, move on to the next.

One by one, accept and surrender every self-limiting belief that you uncovered in the previous session. This does not have to all be done in one session, but make sure you schedule time to move through all these beliefs before moving on to the next session. In the next session, you will reclaim the energy from the old belief and utilize it to propel you forward. However, you cannot reclaim that energy until you have fully released yourself from the old beliefs.

There is no wrong way to do this process, so don't worry about messing it up. Do the best you can and just bring yourself to a place where you feel at peace with letting go of the self-limiting belief. The more you do this, the better you will get at it. Both acceptance and surrender are skills that you only get better at with practice.

Once you have accepted and surrendered all the self-limiting beliefs from the previous session, you can move on to the next level of training.

TRAINING 12
ALIGN YOUR SUBCONSCIOUS PROGRAMMING WITH YOUR VISION

ONGRATULATIONS! YOU HAVE COMPLETED MOST OF the heavy lifting of this process. Now is where you get to reclaim your power by transmuting your old self-limiting beliefs into self-empowering beliefs.

Put on some binaural beats or relaxing meditation instrumental, and let's take back your power.

Once again, open your notes to your list of all your old beliefs.

One by one, you are going to transmute these beliefs so they will work for you instead of against you.

Underneath or next to each old belief, write out "new belief" and try to invert the old belief into a new one that holds the opposite energy. It should look something like this:

"Old belief: I believe I don't have time to work out."

"New belief: I believe I have more than enough time to work out."

"Old belief: I believe I am responsible for making my family happy."

"New belief: I believe I am only responsible for my own happiness."

"Old belief: I believe I am worthless."

"New belief: I believe I am more than enough."

As you begin this process, you will notice that although it's mechanical in nature there is a lot of art involved in being able to transmute the old self-limiting energy into new self-empowering energy.

One thing you want to always consider when writing a new belief is: What are the repercussions of holding this belief? What will it lead to me thinking and doing?

Remember, beliefs are the undercurrents that drive our thoughts and behaviors, so choose wisely. You always want your beliefs to empower you in a way that is in your control. Ultimately, you want to reflect on the outcome you want to create and ask yourself, "What do I need to believe to be true to focus and behave in a way that will get me to that outcome?"

Remember, you create the rules of your own game through the beliefs you hold to be true.

Whatever you believe to be true, you will find a way to make it true as long as you can influence it through your focus and choices.

It makes no sense to believe "I believe I will win the lottery" because there is nothing you can do to influence that outcome in the real world.

Choose beliefs that will transmute the energy that was being held back so it can be reclaimed by your intentional focus and choices.

Now that you have the basic framework down for transmuting your old limiting beliefs into new empowering beliefs, do this for all your old beliefs. Additionally, if you realize you need other beliefs to push you toward your desired outcomes, write those down as well.

When each belief is chosen, close your eyes and breathe it in. Visualize this belief soaking into every cell of your body. Imagine that your identity is shifting internally to incorporate this new belief. Then imagine this new belief takes form on the timeline of your life right in front of you. Visualize a beautiful aura of energy with the colors and emotions aligned with this new belief. Breathe it in, and feel yourself shifting into this new way of being.

When you have completed this exercise for all your new beliefs, you can move onto the next level of training to integrate these beliefs so they are imprinted deep into your subconscious mind now and forever.

Old belief: ....

New belief: ....

Old belief: ....

New belief: ....

Old belief: ....

New belief: ....

Old belief: ....

New belief: ....

Old belief: ....

New belief: ....

Old belief: ....

New belief: ....

Old belief: ....

New belief: ....

Old belief: ....

New belief: ....

Old belief: ....

New belief: ....

Old belief: ....

New belief: ....

Old belief: ....

New belief: ....

Old belief: ....

New belief: ....

Old belief: ....

New belief: ....

Old belief: ....

New belief: ....

Old belief: ....

New belief: ....

INTEGRATE THE NEW YOU

NOW THAT YOUR NEW BELIEFS HAVE been identified and internalized, it is time to make sure this new programming sticks with you. Your subconscious mind learns through repetition and is particularly receptive to new programming when you are in an extremely relaxed state. This relaxed state slows your brainwaves down to the same level they were when you received your initial imprinting during the ages of birth to seven.

As we become adults, our default brainwave activity speeds up, because we are supposed to already have most of the programming we need for survival. The way to slow down our brainwaves to incept these new beliefs is by getting them into our minds when we are in almost a dream-like state.

The best time for this is when you are first waking up in the morning and when you are falling asleep at night. Additionally, you can do progressive relaxation meditations as well to incept these new beliefs while you are relaxed, but the easiest way to do it is by capitalizing on your already receptive mind upon waking up and falling asleep.

RECORD YOUR BELIEF AUDIO

What you will do to incept these new beliefs is record an audio file on your phone, using a voice memo where you read these new beliefs aloud. You then listen to this recorded voice memo every morning and every night when you are in that half-awake half-asleep sleepy state of being.

Make a new list of all your new beliefs you are going to record and then read them all in one recording. The belief audio should be around two to five minutes long, depending on how many beliefs you chose to include.

The reason you use your own voice is obvious. The voice in your head is your voice. The voice that used to talk negatively to you is your voice, so now we are going to flip the script. It only makes sense to use your own voice to incept these new beliefs, because you believe what you hear yourself say.

To make the belief audio as powerful as possible, you will want to record this with the emotional state of believing this to be true already. In other words, bring as much effusive, positive, certain energy to the recording as you can.

Do not go through the motions while recording your belief audio. The more intention, presence, and power you put into the recording, the more powerful it becomes.

State each belief as fact. It is your reality now.

Also, take your time when reading these beliefs and resist the urge to rush and just get it done. Take your time and enjoy the process. That way, whenever you listen to it, you are receiving that same energy with certainty.

The beautiful part of this process is that it's all about you and what you personally need to create the outcomes you desire in your life. I couldn't make a belief audio for you, because it wouldn't be personal, and it wouldn't be as relevant. Only you know what you need to believe to be true to bring your outcomes to reality.

LISTEN TO YOUR BELIEF AUDIO

Listen to this recording every morning and night for the next week. Since your subconscious mind also learns from repetition, feel free to listen to the recording as much as you'd like outside the morning and nightly ritual. The morning and nightly listening is just the bare minimum for reprogramming your subconscious mind with these new beliefs. When you listen more than that, it's bonus points. It will help with the new imprinting even faster.

Don't do anything beyond listening to this for the time being. If you start to have ideas about what actions you want to take, write them down, but refrain from taking action. Next week you will understand why.

One week from now, come back for your next level of training, where we will take your newly aligned subconscious mind and put it to work through new self-empowering habits.

Finally, you can listen to this belief audio for as long as you need until when you hear it the words sound matter-of-fact. In the beginning, you will feel a little resistance toward these new beliefs, and that is 100 percent normal. It takes repetition for your subconscious to shift, so take all the time you need. Only after you get to the point where every belief is received as factual without any resistance can you stop listening.

To get started, listen for one week, and in the next level of training, you will receive additional instructions. Get to it!

TRAINING 14
CHOOSE YOUR HABITS

HOW DOES IT FEEL TO BE you right now?

Notice how the resistance toward your desired outcomes has already started to diminish or may be completely gone already. As mentioned in the last level of training, you should be listening to your belief audio for as long as it takes to feel completely in alignment with these new beliefs. It could take a week, it could take a month, or it could take six months. Trust, honor, and surrender to the process.

Now is the time you have been waiting for. You get to actually take some action.

Bring up all the outcomes you are working toward once again and start to ask yourself, "What would I need to do on a daily or weekly basis to make sure I get to this outcome?"

Sit into that question and then write out every possible thing you could be doing to get to this outcome. Purge out every habit or action that comes to mind under each of these outcomes.

Once you have done so for every outcome, go back to each list and ask yourself, "Given what you know to be true, what would be the most impactful actions I could take to get to this outcome?"

There will be things that you are already doing that you need to continue, and there will be new things that come to mind that you weren't already doing. Only you know the level of action necessary to get you where you want to go.

The key is to not overload yourself with new habits. Choose one to three new habits to add to your game plan as it relates to each of these outcomes that you know will bring you closer to your outcome if you stay consistent with them.

Here is what this could look like:

Outcome: 190 pounds, six-pack abs
Habits: Work out five times a week for thirty minutes, track my food intake daily and hit my calorie goal, get minimum of eight hours of sleep a night.

You are literally reverse engineering your outcomes by picking habits that you know or at least believe will give you the best shot at getting to your outcome.

If you are thinking to yourself, *I don't know what will get me to my outcome*, turn off your thinking mind and ask yourself, *If I could get to this outcome, how would I do it? What would I need to do? How often would I need to do it? Where would I start?*

This may not be the complete blueprint for getting you to the outcome, but the fact that you are choosing actions to execute on will bring you into a state of momentum that will eventually lead to you choosing the right actions. Like getting to any goal, the path will very likely not be linear. You will try things. Some things will work better than others. Stay curiously diligent on your path to identifying the best actions.

If you are already at a very high level in your chosen discipline, the actions required will be obvious now that you have cleared out the resistance. If you are a beginner trying to figure something out for the first time, you will need to seek out the answers and try different things until you find success. Oftentimes, we have no idea what will move the needle until we start taking action. Don't be afraid to fail. View every failure as an opportunity to learn and grow. Everything that doesn't work is a valuable piece of data because you are narrowing down what you should try to do. Stay curious. Keep learning. Keep growing. You will find your way.

Once you have your habits or actions listed out that you believe will get you to your desired outcome, move on to the next level of training, where I will help you put together a sustainable system to implement these habits.

Outcome: ....

Habits: ....

Outcome: ....

Habits: ....

Outcome: ....

Habits: ....

Outcome: ....

Habits: ....

Outcome: ....

Habits: ....

Outcome: ....

Habits: ....

Outcome: ....

Habits: ....

Outcome: ....

Habits: ....

Outcome: ....

Habits: ....

Outcome: ....

Habits: ....

Outcome: ....

Habits: ....

SYSTEMIZE YOUR SUCCESS

ONGRATULATIONS ONCE AGAIN FOR IDENTIFYING THE actions necessary to bring you closer to your desired outcomes. Now we will begin the process of systemizing these actions so they stick long-term.

PICK A FOCUS

What I have seen in my life and the life of my clients is that not everything can be the main thing. You will need to have one area of your life that is the top priority you will put above all the rest for at least a season. A season could be three- or six-month periods of time.

During this time, you put the other areas of your life into maintenance mode. You do just enough to sustain your results or move them forward just a bit. The truth is your energy and time are finite, so making the main thing the main thing will be important for seeing physical results in your world. You can't do everything at once, but you can do damn near anything if you focus your energy.

Right now, choose your main focus, and then each week when you schedule your calendar and to-do list tasks, keep it in mind when prioritizing your schedule.

BLOCKS OF TIME: CALENDAR

The first tool you are going to use is your calendar. Schedule every new habit or recurring action into your calendar so you are forced to give it the space you need to execute on it. Since your obligations from week to week may vary, I recommend scheduling your calendar work for the week ahead on the same day each week. I do this on Monday mornings. Pick a day that works best for you.

Here is what this can look like for you. For the fitness outcome, you would just schedule five one-hour blocks into your calendar. That way, you don't steamroll through your day without executing on the most important habits that will bring you closer to your outcome.

Right now, review all the habits or actions you are committed to and create space in your calendar for each of these, if it's applicable.

FLUID ACTIONS: TO-DO LIST TRACKER

For the habits or actions that are more fluid, like tracking your food intake, you will need a second tool: a to-do list tracker. You will create recurring daily or weekly to-do list tasks that you have to check off to bring awareness to whether you are doing each task or not.

Don't go crazy with the tech. Any simple to-do list tracker will do. I like to use a piece of software called Asana. On there, I include everything (that is not already on my calendar) that I want a task to check off to confirm whether I have done it or not.

Again, don't overthink this. Simply observe your habits that you know you want to be consistent with and then schedule them in your calendar and/or on a to-do list tracker. What you are aiming to do here is create a sustainable lifestyle that includes the habits that will reverse engineer the outcomes you desire.

As you start doing this week over week, you will be able to better identify what you have the bandwidth for, and you can prioritize accordingly.

Now that you've got your game plan scheduled, execute it for a week, and then dive into the final section of training.

TRAINING 16
LIVE YOUR LIFE IN FLOW

Y OU MADE IT! IT IS TIME to play the infinite game of life. Although you have just completed this training, the journey has just begun. You now know that there are only two things in your control. Your focus and your choices.

If you can own those two things by utilizing the tools in this training, you will continue to clean up your inner planet and own the outcomes of your life.

So much of our energy is expended trying to control the uncontrollable. As I mentioned at the outset, embracing this new way of being makes you abnormal. Most people are living reactively. Embracing the tools to continue to reprogram your subconscious mind for success will empower you to live presently in your power. When you commit to this path, your consciousness levels will rise, and you will be in communion with the Oneness—feeling yourself being guided by a higher power that has your best interest.

The truth is that when you are fully aligned at the subconscious level, you will create the exact opportunities that are best for you at that moment in time. It may not be on the timeline you want, but it is the timeline you need. What's for you can't be taken from you. Trust that what leaves you will come back to you in time if it's meant to be. If it doesn't, it was not meant for you. Forcing things will not bring you the results that you desire. They will only result in frustration and a lower emotional frequency. Your power comes from stepping into what is showing up in your life right now. Trust that what's right in front of you right now has a purpose, and it needs your full attention if you want to move toward the next level of your development.

As you learn to become meditation, you will start living in your truth without tethers. When I talk about becoming meditation, I mean that you are fully aware of your inner emotional experience in the present moment and how you are creating it through your conscious and subconscious focus. When you have these skills at your disposal, you are able to change the way you feel on command. This is the most valuable skill you will ever learn. It's one thing to be able to meditate in silence to bring yourself back into a peaceful state of being. It's another to be able to do it in real time in the middle of chaos. That is what becomes available to you when you become meditation.

I hope by learning about my story and learning these actionable tools, you feel empowered to live your life on your terms. It's time to stop acting out of obligation and embrace who you are.

That is what we need as a planet and as a species now more than ever.

Your value is not based on what you do. It's a byproduct of who you are. The deep down essence of you.

Here is how you can embrace this path going forward.

Live your life from a space of curiosity, wonder, and alignment with your own self-defined truth.

Understand that you are already who you need to be. The subconscious self-limiting programming is the only thing you need to clear away to reveal the potential of who you could be.

Play the infinite game in a way where you trust that as long as you are continuing to move through the resistance on the subconscious level, you will be guided exactly where you need to be.

As you strive to be and achieve more, you will undoubtedly be met with new challenges.

My hope is that you now feel like you have the necessary tools to transcend those challenges and keep growing toward your highest potential.

You were born for a reason: to find joy while harnessing your unique talents in the present moment. There is no right way to do life. You only know what you're doing is right when you feel lost in the present moment, experiencing flow in the task at hand.

That is what the infinite game is all about—finding and following your flow.

Best case scenario for me is that you gain so much mastery over your feelings and outcomes that you have the courage to one day surrender fully to this feeling of flow. Trusting that the innate power flowing through you and the joy you experience in the present moment is the most meaningful compass to follow.

Once you have done this through reprogramming yourself for success, that is where the real game of life begins.

Thank you from the bottom of my heart for embracing this journey with me.

If there is ever an opportunity for us to work together in any capacity, it would be my greatest honor to be your guide.

Own your focus. Own your choices. Own your life.

With love,
Brandon

ACKNOWLEDGEMENTS

I WOULD LIKE TO ACKNOWLEDGE AND SHARE MY APPRECIATION FOR all my mentors, friends, family and clients that have been a part of my journey up until this point. To Sensei Clay for starting me down this path and equipping me with powerful tools to heal myself and others. To my coach Keyen Lage who was instrumental in helping me step fully into my power. To my wife and daughters, Sara, Mar and Luna who are the center of my world. To all my coaching clients who have trusted me as their guide on their own personal journeys. To my parents Benj and Joann who have always given me unconditional love and support. To my friends who have been there with me throughout my journey, you know who you are. To the team at Scribe Media, without you this book in its final form would not have been possible. Thank you.

ABOUT THE AUTHOR

Brandon Epstein was a college football player turned mental performance coach to some of the most elite athletes and entrepreneurs in the world. After riding the bench his freshman year playing football he uncovered his hidden potential through the field of mental performance. This led to a successful college football career, a bachelor's degree in The Mental Aspect of Human Performance and being a recepient of the Fletcher's Jones

He helps high achievers turn inner resistance into inner power for career best performances. He has over 15 years working in the space and his clients range from millionaire entrepreneurs, to creative artists, to athletes ranging from Pro Boxing, to Pro MMA, to the NFL, to the MLB, to name a few. He is also an entrepreneur who has built businesses that have empowered millions of people around the world to be their best selves through his educational content. Brandon is a devoted husband and father. Finally, he is a seeker of truth humbly on the path of personal awakening.

Contact me
Instagram *@brandonepstein_*
Email *brandon@theowned.industries*
Website *https://thebrandonepstein.com/*

Apply for one on one coaching at
https://www.theowned.industries/coaching

Made in United States
Troutdale, OR
10/05/2024